Resolve rounds out a great series on church history as seen through the eyes of those who were there. Covering the last two centuries, Davis uses the stories of modern Christian leaders to show how the present day church continues to evangelize, train pastors, and confront social issues. Readers will learn much from the short biographies and be encouraged that the cause of Christ continues around the world.

Linda Finlayson
Author

Davis guides his reader through the decades and across continents as he transcends denominational divides to craft a tapestry of Kingdom influencers who point the reader to the importance of the gospel, its reasonableness, relevance, and defense today ... an excellent resource for anyone, not just young people.

Thomas Foley
Founder, Christian Educators Outreach;
Pastor, Mt. Shiloh Baptist Church, Faber, Virginia

Luke Davis' final volume brings the story of the Church into modern times. Here we meet with some familiar saints, such as B.B. Warfield, C.S. Lewis, Corrie Ten Boom, Dietrich Bonhoeffer, and J.I. Packer, and others less well-known, all woven into a rich tapestry of God's glory. As with Luke's other volumes, this is a grand introduction to the modern era. I commend it warmly.

Nick Needham
Church history tutor,
Highland Theological College, Scotland

In the great tradition of teaching history through story, Luke Davis's final volume in the Risen Hope Series, *The Enduring Church*, brings to life sig

hundred years of the Church. With vividness and delight, these stories not only indicate the major contributions of the subjects but do so while presenting remarkable features of their personalities and practices. The happy result is that readers receive something more like mentoring than a mere historical profile. I happily recommend these volumes, but especially for young readers who need to see that History need not be a dull subject; rather, it can be the telling of the wonderful ways God has used ordinary people to do extraordinary things.

Rev. Dr. Benjamin Fischer (PhD, Notre Dame)
Associate Professor of Literature, Northwest
Nazarene University
Rector, Christ the Redeemer Anglican Church

RESOLVE

THE CHURCH THAT ENDURES ONWARD

LUKE H. DAVIS

CF4·K

10 9 8 7 6 5 4 3 2

Copyright © 2024 Luke H. Davis
Paperback ISBN: 978-1-5271-1106-6
Ebook ISBN: 978-1-5271-1125-7

Published by Christian Focus Publications,
Geanies House, Fearn, Tain, Ross-shire,
IV20 1TW, Scotland, U.K.
www.christianfocus.com;
email: info@christianfocus.com

Design and illustrations: Laura K. Sayers
Cover designer: Catriona Mackenzie

Printed and bound by
Bell and Bain, Glasgow

Scripture quotations are from The Holy Bible, English
Standard Version, copyright © 2001 by Crossway Bibles,
a publishing ministry of Good News Publishers. Used by
permission. All rights reserved. ESV Text Edition: 2011.

CONTENTS

DEDICATED WITH LOVE TO

Victoria Anne Davis
a.k.a., our precious granddaughter Tori

May the Savior who resolved to build His Church
be the One to Whom you call out,
and as you endure onward,
may you place your trusting heart
in His loving, nail-scarred hands.

IMPORTANT MOMENTS
FOR THE ENDURING CHURCH

1880
J.C. Ryle is consecrated as Bishop of Liverpool

1887
B.B. Warfield begins teaching theology at Princeton Seminary

1893
Samuel Morris dies in Fort Wayne, Indiana

1925
Francis Grimke retires as pastor of the Fifteenth Street Presbyterian Church in Washington, D.C.

1931
C.S. Lewis becomes a Christian

1937
Dietrich Bonhoeffer's *The Cost of Discipleship* is published

1944
Corrie ten Boom is arrested by the Gestapo for sheltering Jews and Kaj Munk is killed by Nazis in Denmark

1945
Nazis hang Dietrich Bonhoeffer to death at Flossenburg, Germany

1947
Billy Graham preaches his first crusade in Grand Rapids, Michigan

1952
C.S. Lewis' *Mere Christianity* is published in Great Britain

1955
Francis and Edith Schaeffer begin their L'Abri ministry in Switzerland

1956
Jim Elliot and four other missionaries are murdered in Eduador

1963
Martin Luther King gives his memorable 'I Have a Dream' speech in Washington, D.C.

1968
David Martyn Lloyd-Jones retires as pastor of Westminster Chapel
in London

1973
J.I. Packer publishes his classic book, *Knowing God*

1974
Billy Graham and John Stott lead the Lausanne World Evangelization
Conference in Switzerland

1975
E.K. Bailey helps establish Concord Missionary Baptist Church
in Dallas

1983
Eta Linneman moves to Indonesia to train pastors in Batu

1989
Tim Keller founds Redeemer Presbyterian Church in New York City

2007
Ben Kwashi survives an attack by Islamic soldiers in his home

2016
J. Alec Motyer dies in England

2018
Asia Noreen Bibi is acquitted of blasphemy charges in Pakistan

THE ENDURING CHURCH

On the night before His death, Jesus gathered his disciples together (minus Judas, who was busy betraying the Lord) to speak with them about some urgent matters. The apostle John gives us considerable detail about what Jesus said, but possibly the most striking element of the whole night is that—as Jesus was facing His own agonizing sacrificial death the next day—He informed his friends about what they would face in the future.

> If the world hates you, know that it has hated me before it hated you. If you were of the world, the world would love you as its own; but because you are not of the world, but I chose you out of the world, therefore the world hates you. Remember the word that I said to you: "A servant is not greater than his master." If they persecute me, they will also persecute you.[1]

If there was one thing that marked the disciples' experience after Jesus' death and resurrection, it was that they had to endure many troubles and trials. This came true in those early years of the church (which I have covered in the first volume in this series, *Redemption: The Church in Ancient Times*). Over many years, Christianity grew to become a larger force in society (the Middle Ages), then fractured and had to rebuild itself (the Protestant Reformation), and then expand further around the world. Now we have been living in an age that is more secular, less religious, and—in some cases— more hostile to the Gospel of Jesus Christ. What was old is new again. Jesus calls his followers to endure hardship.

1. John 15:18-20a (ESV)

This is not to say one's life is automatically in constant danger—though as Christians we should be prepared for that possibility. However, followers of Jesus should be willing and ready to endure trials and hardships. And we will see that through many of the personalities depicted in this book.

Sammy Morris endured hardship in Africa before encountering Jesus and seeking an opportunity to train as a missionary to return to Liberia. B.B. Warfield was a faithful professor who dutifully and lovingly cared for his wife who was an invalid. C.S. Lewis was a profound Christian thinker who had to battle against the secularization of British society and later endured the death of his wife, Joy, from cancer. Francis Grimke endured the racism of American society. Dietrich Bonhoeffer and Corrie ten Boom stared down the savage evil of the Nazis in the Second World War. Eta Linneman and J.I. Packer had to confront a devaluing of Scripture from professing Christians in their own contexts. And Benjamin Kwashi and his family barely escaped with their lives as they are ongoing targets of Islamic terror and violence. The Church endures forward. But by God's grace, it does endure.

There is a plaque in the lobby of a building in Philadelphia, Pennsylvania that I have been thinking about more and more as the end of this project drew near. The building is called the Palestra, and it is where the University of Pennsylvania plays its basketball games. The plaque reads as follows:

> To win the game is great
> To play the game is greater
> But to love the game is the greatest of all.

Writing this series of church history stories has filled me with a great deal of joy, because I have had a chance to share the work of God through His people in history with you, the readers. That has been a process both uplifting and humbling. To write stories of the history of the Church—in both its blessedness and blemishes—is to partake of a thrilling journey that is helped by the fact that I absolutely adore writing. To paraphrase Eric Lidell in the movie *Chariots of Fire,* when I write, I feel God's pleasure. And so I can truly say, as I finish these volumes, that to imagine the story is great, to write the story is greater still, but to love the story is the greatest of all.

And where I find greatest joy is that the Savior who is the subject of the Great Story writes the story of my life by His grace.

Luke H. Davis
Pentecost 2023

SAMMY MORRIS

March 1893, Fort Wayne, Indiana

The bed shook violently. Yet, even in the darkness and with the storm crashing around outside, the young man knew the weather had nothing to do with the rattling of his bed. That was due to his coughing, which had become more frequent and brutal over the past month. The cold that he had caught in December had taken on a life of its own, becoming more and more severe. Though the temperature outside was cool and the window was open, Sammy felt his head and knew the fever wasn't leaving him anytime soon. Every cough, indeed every bodily movement, was a descent into physical anguish.

Close your eyes, he told himself, *and pretend you are anywhere but here.* That was a trick he would play on his mind, knowing that distraction from any agony would help him fall asleep. At least, that was the usual practice. Play tricks on the mind. He felt his eyelids grow heavy as his body was racked with another round of coughing.

He never thought that he was entering a moment when his own mind would play tricks on him. He yawned after another cough and suddenly he was in Africa just five years before. Known by a different name. And scared.

Kaboo felt the sting in his side where the soldier's foot had just punted him in the ribs. The man's staff came down hard, nearly crushing Kaboo's cheekbone, bringing laughter from the other soldiers assembled there in the copse of trees.

"You felt that one, didn't you, little prince?" taunted Kaboo's assailant. He reached down and pulled the boy up by his ear before smashing his forearm across Kaboo's nose. A flow of blood escaped and began traveling down Kaboo's face and dripped off his chin as the warriors around him howled with laughter.

"That's what comes of being royalty in a tribe that cannot afford to even see their little prince!" another man guffawed loudly as Kaboo slumped to the ground. The soldiers were beside themselves with laughter, never noticing that the prince peered upward as he gagged and sputtered, seeing a narrow path in the distance leading away from the tribe's village. *If only,* thought the prince to himself, *if only I could get there without being seen.* The words had barely coursed through his mind when another strike to the back of his head nearly made him unconscious. The howls of laughter grew around him, and he tried and failed to push himself off the ground. He felt rough hands pulling him up anyway and then a rope being tightened around his hands. Slowly, his feet went a few inches clear of the ground. He looked up and saw the rope was tightened around a tree branch. He looked downward and saw the Grebo chief glaring up at him.

"Pathetic little pawn," the chief spat. "Stupid little Kru." And he punched him as hard as he could in the stomach.

Kaboo gasped for breath as the soldiers walked off with their chief, laughing all the way as they drifted out of sight. Kaboo coughed and felt the searing pain in his abdomen when he looked up and saw it.

Bright light through the night sky.

And a voice. Directed at him.

"Kaboo! Flee!"

"He was coughing terribly, sir," said the student, opening the door of Sammy's room with one hand and holding the candlestick in his other. Stepping past him in the room was a thin man with a high forehead, already shedding his coat and then rubbing his white goateed beard that dripped past his chin. Kneeling at Sammy's bed, he placed his coat on top of the blanket and said, "Sammy? Sammy. It's President Reade[1]. Wayne heard you in some distress and went outside to get help and I happened to be passing by the dormitory. I am here."

Sammy turned his head from his pillow, scarcely believing that his teacher was there in the room with him. "Reverend Reade!" he exclaimed through coughs that battered his body. "I should apologize for causing both you and my friend Mr. Berry here any fright."

"You will do no such thing," said Reade, taking Sammy's hand. "Wayne did right by alerting me. We want to make sure you have the chance to get well. It's distressing that this cold has afflicted you for this long."

"It isn't a cold anymore, Reverend Reade," Sammy sputtered. "It is pneumonia, and it doesn't seem to be getting any better. In fact, I feel worse physically every passing day. I spoke to the doctor who came from the infirmary and he said there is little, if anything, that can be done."

Reade's face fell, as if he was hearing his own sentence of death. "You are certain, Prince Kaboo? You are absolutely sure?"

Sammy nodded.

"Excuse me," Wayne interrupted. "Did I hear you correctly that you called him Kaboo? Prince Kaboo?"

Reade looked at Wayne incredulously, but Sammy waved dismissively. "It is fine, Reverend Reade. Wayne has only been here since September. He doesn't know all my story."

"All these times, you have prayed with me," gushed Wayne, "and you never told me you were a prince?"

---

1. "Reade" is Rev. Thaddeus Reade, who was the president of Taylor University (at this time located in Fort Wayne, Indiana) from 1891-1902. A Methodist minister and hymnwriter, he was instrumental in moving the campus to the small town of Upland, Indiana, later in 1893.

Before Sammy could answer, Reade placed his hand on Sammy's forehead. "Sammy," he said gravely, "you have a fever. Wayne will stay here with you, while I go to fetch some medicine for you."

"It will only prolong the inevitable, sir," Sammy said through a grimace, "but some temporary relief would be enjoyable. That way Wayne and I can talk and I can tell him who I really am."

President Reade nodded his agreement and tapped Wayne on his shoulder. "I'll be right back, but I have a feeling you'll be a completely different man when I return."

Wayne placed the candle on the end table and sat on the bed as Sammy gathered himself and leaned against the wall with the blanket around him, shivering from the fever.

"What Reverend Reade said is true," Sammy began. "My original name was Kaboo, and I was a prince in Liberia, son of the chief of the Kru tribe, a proud people. But one day some six years ago, a neighboring tribe attacked mine, and I was captured. They used me as ransom, but they had no intention of returning me, even if my father paid enough. They allowed my family to visit me but when my tribe could no longer pay the ransom fees, the beatings began and over time they got worse. Finally, one day, my captors left me hanging in a tree and I looked into the sky. A bright light shone directly in my eyes and I heard someone tell me to flee."

Wayne remained silent as Sammy endured another coughing fit. "My only escape was through the jungle. I didn't know where I was going, and to truly survive and not bring harm to my family, I would have to leave behind my past life forever. I stumbled through the jungle at night since it was not likely I'd be seen in the dark. During the day I would find a hollowed-out tree and hide for hours. I endured insect bites and my body was covered in grazes and cuts. My diet was nothing like what we get in our meals here!"

"No chicken or potatoes?" Wayne asked, attempting to lighten the mood.

"More like mangoes and snails," Sammy replied, clutching his chest as he stifled another cough. "Finally, I happened upon a coffee plantation near the coast, and the owner took pity upon me."

"I'm just relieved he never returned you to the cruel tribe," Wayne said. "In the past in Indiana, slaves from the Southern states were often returned to their owners, sad to say."

"No," said Sammy. "The owner was a kind and generous man who cared for his workers. In fact, overseeing the work was a former slave from America. He'd gained his freedom and had moved to Liberia. Part of my living arrangement there was a requirement to attend church, so I would go to services each week at a church which was led by missionaries. One day, the man was preaching from the story in Acts ... you know, the one where Saul is pursuing the Christians and is on the outskirts of Damascus, ready to go in there, arrest them and imprison them. But God intervened! And it was through a bright light that he changed Saul's life, and he became Paul and a great proclaimer of the Gospel! And I thought, why, that is much like the bright light I saw in the sky, I remembered the voice I had heard. It was a voice from heaven. I believed God was calling me to Himself through his Son, Jesus Christ. And so I, Prince Kaboo, a runaway, came home to the arms of my Savior."

"So why do they call you Sammy Morris now?" Wayne inquired, the candle's flame flickering in the room.

Sammy hacked and coughed again, nearly falling off the bed but regaining his balance. "Later, I was baptized there at the church so that people might see I was committing myself to Jesus and to whatever He might call me to do.

During my time at the church, one of the missionaries there befriended me and taught me God's Word. As a tribute to him, I took his name as my new name at baptism. Before God shone the light of Jesus into my heart, I was Prince Kaboo. Afterward, I became Sammy Morris. That was the missionary's name. And it is my name today."

"But how did you end up here at Taylor?"

"That," Sammy uttered after yet another coughing fit of about a minute, "was truly the work of God. Mr. Morris told me about a Bible teacher in New York, a Stephen Merritt, who was well-connected and could provide me with an opportunity to find a place to learn more about the Bible. So I said, 'That's it. I'm going to New York!' I found a ship willing to take me over as long as I paid my fare by working aboard. It was not the best of circumstances. Members of the crew were savage and beat me terribly, but again I heard that voice of God, this time telling me to endure. And do you know what? I endured their insults and their beatings, and I verbally forgave them. They were stunned, and for a while they continued with their beatings. But one day we travelled through a dangerous storm on the Atlantic Ocean and, although they were certain we all would die, they saw me praying quietly through it all. One of them asked me, 'Why aren't you afraid?' I told him and the rest of the crew, 'Because I have Jesus. I have peace. The storm is part of what we endure. But Jesus is greater than all the storms we endure.' And from that moment on, they were asking me to pray with them, for them, to tell them about Jesus. Many of them placed their faith in Jesus, and by the time we docked in New York, the ship crew was a new group of men from the ones who had left the port in Liberia."

"And you ended up finding Dr. Merritt in New York?" continued Reade, who had returned with a bottle of medicine.

"I did, sir," said Sammy, holding his hands out for the pills as he reached for a glass of water at the bedside. "Stephen was very instrumental in taking me in—at a time when a number of people criticized him for giving lodging to a black man—and then raising enough money to send me here. This, Reverend Reade … this, Wayne … this has been my dream. To come and learn about Jesus even more. To love him more. And to study His Word, for the purpose of returning to my home country to preach Christ to the people there, so that King Jesus might reign there." He coughed again, more violently than before, and then used all his energy to attempt sitting up. Even then, he needed Reade and Wayne to help him. "It has been a wonderful dream. I am sad it will not be fulfilled, but God will direct others to Africa in my stead."

"What do you mean?" blurted out Wayne, suddenly crestfallen. He looked at President Reade. "What does Sammy mean by that?"

Reade frowned. "I confirmed with the university doctor what Sammy already knows. It is not a severe cold any longer. It is pneumonia. And it is slowly taking our friend Sammy." Reade wiped a tear away from his eye. "I should be comforted that you will be in the presence of our Lord Jesus, Sammy, but …" and his voice broke, " … it is still so sad."

"Reverend Reade," Sammy said, his voice suddenly and inexplicably stronger now, "it is not my work any longer to go back to Liberia. It is Jesus' work. I am finishing my work. I have lived my dream. How could I not be overjoyed when Jesus has saved me and given me the opportunity to love Him more during my brief sojourn in this world? I have drunk deeply of His Scriptures! I have been able to pray with and encourage countless students here at Taylor. It is my work no longer. Jesus will send others better than I to bring His Word to Africa."

Wayne's tears were coursing down his face. "I was one of those students, Sammy," he said, his hands shaking as he laid one of them on Sammy's hand. "I was here in September and wandering around the buildings. I was in a moment of fright and wondered if I would really succeed. What purpose did God have for me being here? And then you rounded the corner near the administration building, and you saw me in great distress. You approached me and said, 'Brother, I want to pray for you.' And you did. You prayed as naturally as it is for people to breathe. Right there, you placed your hand on my head and spoke words of comfort and strength over me. I can't even remember what you said. But when you said 'Amen', I knew God was with me, and that I was strong for the tasks ahead. And you have not stopped praying for me or others since then."

Wayne looked at Sammy, who had leaned against him, eyes closed, his breathing slowed near the point of sleep. Reade approached the bed and helped ease Sammy down on his mattress and bade Wayne to come with him. He shut the door and the two men made their way down the corridor.

"I'll get the nurse to check on him," Reade said, "but we must prepare ourselves that it might not be long. God is calling him home." He looked sideways at Wayne. "Are you all right, Mr. Berry?"

"I am," Wayne said, his face aglow with hope. "Like you said, after being with Sammy, I will never be the same again."

SAMUEL KABOO MORRIS left his tumultuous life in Liberia with Christ in his heart and joy in every step. His passionate and infectious faith made impact on nearly everyone he encountered, but it was his conviction that his Liberian countrymen needed to know Jesus that drove him to be trained as a missionary. At Taylor University, Sammy would offer to pray for fellow students, and many spoke of what an encouragement he was to them. Newspapers in northern Indiana printed stories of the lad from Africa "who was changing Fort Wayne with the power of God." His return to Liberia, however, was not to be, as a severe cold he contracted in late 1892 turned into pneumonia early the next year. On May 12, 1893, the twenty-year-old Morris finally died and entered into his eternal reward. His life inspired a number of his classmates to become missionaries to Africa, and his faithful endeavors continue to be felt in the Taylor University community, which has erected a statue in his likeness and named one of their dormitories Samuel Morris Hall.

J.C. RYLE

September 1896, St. Luke's Church-Walton, Liverpool, England

"I'll be glad when the weather clears in advance of the weekend," said the factory worker as he turned right and stomped along Spellow Lane going eastward. His fellow laborer struggled to keep up with him.

"I don't understand what's the rush," uttered his friend Jimmy as his lungs felt they were enduring a house fire. "Even if there's a line at that chip shop, we'll be back on the shift in plenty of time."

"Not that, Jimmy," grumbled the worker, wrinkling his nose and stifling a wet cough. "On Wednesdays, there's a free lunch at the church up here after a left and a quick trot. I'd rather pay nothing for my food than pass over my hard-earned money."

"Which church is that?" asked Jimmy.

"St. Luke's, Walton, it is," hacked the friend. "You get a bowl of soup and a thick slice o'bread with a mug of tea. All you have to do is sit there while the rector preaches at you for fifteen minutes. I figure we can do that and rush back before lunch break is over."

Jimmy's boots, tied too tightly again as he liked his laces extra snug, were hurting his feet, but he didn't want to turn down the chance of a free meal in the middle of the day. "I don't care much for darkening the door of a church, but food is food." They made the left turn as they saw the structure of Goodison Park rise to their right. Beyond that, Jimmy saw there was indeed a church tucked in near the end of the football stand. "Here we go" he said, "quick soup and bread and dash away. Do we really have to stay for someone to preach at us?"

Later, Jimmy would reflect on the irony of that question. For the moment, he trudged on, unaware he was heading toward a moment that would change his life.

"Keep going, keep going, move the line along," said the woman ladling the soup into bowl after bowl. "There you go, son, to the end of the line and get your bread. Find a place and the speaker will begin in just a minute."

Jimmy staggered to his table, trying to gently balance the chicken and potato broth in his hands so that the bread would not submerge below its thick surface. But upon arriving at the table, he saw his friend was gobbling down the last of his soup and stuffing the bread in his tattered pocket.

"What are you doing?" Jimmy insisted. "You look as if you're about to sneak out the side door!"

"Which is exactly what I am about to do, if you'll keep your voice down!"

Jimmy looked away, certain that others were noticing their strident conversation. When he looked back, his friend had disappeared.

"Now what?" grumbled Jimmy as he slumped into his chair and hovered over his soup and bread.

"Hello, sir?" came the voice above him and to the left. "May I sit down with you to eat?"

Jimmy looked up, surprised that anyone would think him good company for lunch, and he saw a gentle-faced bearded man, dressed neatly in a black shirt with matching trousers. He held a massive dark brown leather book in one hand and a bowl of soup in the other. A slice of bread wobbled on the soup's surface, partly obscuring the spoon within the bowl. Jimmy was surprised to see someone so neatly dressed willing to sit with an ordinary bloke such as himself. This gentlemen also looked to be at least eighty years old. Why was he desiring his company at lunchtime?

"By all means," said the surprised Jimmy. "I wasn't sure if you were a regular here or not."

"Not so," said his table visitor, "at least not at St. Luke's, but I am a resident of Liverpool, so I am familiar with the territory. Do you come here often for lunch?"

"No, this is my first time," Jimmy replied and then, surprising himself with his own graciousness, extended his hand. "My name is Jimmy. Didn't mean to keep you from your soup, but wanted to introduce myself."

"Thank you, Jimmy. My name is John," came the response, before his companion said, "and as for the soup, if you'll indulge me one moment."

And he bowed his head, closing his eyes and muttered words that Jimmy couldn't make out, but which sounded earnest and sincere. After a few moments, John straightened himself and tore a hunk from his slice of bread.

"Your first time here at St. Luke's for either lunch or church, is that so?" John asked him.

"Never noticed it was tucked away here," said Jimmy. "I work at the toffee factory just beyond Spellow Lane southwest of here. The closest I've gotten to this church is the rare time I'm able to come up to Goodison Park for a football match."

"You're an Everton supporter, are you?" John asked, his eyes dancing.

"Yes, cheer on the Blues, I do," Jimmy smiled, glad that a man of John's age was willing to talk football in a place where Jimmy feared religion would be the verbal currency. "I like our chances this year, I think. Would love to win the First Division title, but we have to get past Aston Villa to do that. Still, getting Jack Taylor over from St. Mirren should help our chances. D'you follow Everton, sir?"

"No, I am often too busy to speak knowledgably about football," John replied, deflating Jimmy's hopes for an extended chat about sport. "However, I know John Houlding, the founder of Liverpool Football Club, so if I had to choose one to follow, it might be them."

Ugh, Liverpool! thought Jimmy. *How can anyone support the Reds?* He was hopeful that his face did not betray any disgust, but John was already standing from the table after only a few nibbles at his soup. "I say, John, are you leaving before the preacher gets up there?"

"Not in the least" John replied, his eyes twinkling, "and the rector isn't here today."

"How do you know that?" Jimmy inquired before putting another spoonful of soup in his mouth. But John was already headed to a makeshift lectern, fifteen feet away.

"Good afternoon!" John's voice boomed through the parish hall, catching the attention of the twenty scattered over several tables. "I hope you are warm and comfortable, and that the food is especially filling. I should introduce myself. I am John, although my friends and churchgoers usually know me as J.C., that's J.C. Ryle. I happen to be the bishop[1] for the Church of England parishes here in the Liverpool area, and as I received word that the vicar[2] of St. Luke's was taken ill and would not be available for the lunch message today, I volunteered in his stead."

Jimmy nearly choked on his bread! *The bishop,* he nearly gasped aloud. *I was speaking with the bishop himself? A common grubby worker like me talking to the bishop?*

"For the moment," Bishop John continued, "let us pause from our meal. I will be brief enough that your soup will

---

1. In the Church of England, a bishop is a minister who has responsibility for overseeing the clergy and churches in a given region, which is called a diocese.
2. A vicar is one of several titles for ministers in the Church of England. In this case, the vicar would be the sole pastor of a church.

remain warm and digestible after my short talk, but I would urge you to recognize that giving me your undivided attention now would benefit you later. Thank you."

Jimmy was sure that guffaws and chuckles would follow Bishop John's request, but to his great surprise, he heard the clatters of spoons as the rough-looking contingent of men gathered there dropped their utensils on the tables, their attention rooted on the bishop. What surprised Jimmy even more was that he did the same! *What is this? His very presence seems to command respect from everyone here,* Jimmy thought.

"I would like to bring those of you here into a moment from the earthly life of Jesus Christ," Bishop John went on. "This is from the Gospel of Mark, the tenth chapter, and in this event, we discover someone who is bold enough to ask a question I imagine many of you, in your honest moments, are willing to ask, as well. God's Word says this: *And when he was gone forth into the way, there came one running, and kneeled to him, and asked him, 'Good Master, what shall I do that I may inherit eternal life?' And Jesus said unto him, 'Why callest thou me good? There is none that is good but one, that is, God. Thou knowest the commandments, Do not commit adultery, Do not kill, Do not steal, Do not bear false witness, Defraud not, Honor thy father and mother.' And he answered and said unto him, 'Master, all these have I observed from my youth.' Then Jesus, beholding him, loved him, and said unto him, 'One thing thou lackest: Go thy way, sell whatsoever thou hast, and give to the poor, and thou shalt have treasure in heaven: and come, take up the cross, and follow me.' And he was sad at that saying, and went away grieved: for he had many possessions.*"[3]

Straightening himself at the lectern, Bishop John looked out at the twenty or so men gathered at the tables. "I shall not keep you long, for I know some of you need to return to your places of labor. But the moment is urgent, and I would

3. This is from Mark 10:17-22. As J.C. Ryle referred to the King James Version text of the Bible in his writings, it is safe to assume he would use it in his speech.

not be doing my duty if I did not present two chief lessons for you to carry in your souls from this day forth."

"The first lesson that I wish to press upon you men is how self-ignorant we can be. See the man who comes running to Jesus and kneels before him! He carries a spirit of need, of seriousness about him, otherwise why would he run to Jesus? And he asks the question of questions, 'What must I do to inherit eternal life?' Think on that, men! Don't you wish to live forever? Don't you desire to live in the presence of God and know nothing but his joy and all goodness forever and ever?"

Jimmy found himself agreeing with the bishop's sentiments. His speech, his turns of phrase were so clear and direct that Jimmy couldn't help being drawn in.

"And yet," the bishop, raising an open palm, said, "this man claims he has done what is required when Jesus reminds him of God's requirements: 'All these have I observed from my youth.' All this time the man is woefully ignorant of his own heart! He might not have committed adultery, but lust surely dwelt in his heart. He might not have murdered, but how often did unjust anger erupt from within? You men here today, perhaps you have never stolen an item from a shop, but how often have you, by not working diligently in your position, robbed your employers of the full quality of your labor? Even in the moments you do not lie to another person, do you not consider how to avoid being fully truthful? You might say, 'I am only a humble laborer', and that may be true, but does that prevent you from coveting and desiring the possessions of others that are not yours to take? We are all self-ignorant of our sin; this penetrating word is for us all."

Then Jimmy noticed the bishop's face transform into a kindly form, set with a hopeful smile. "And yet," Bishop John continued, "let us see another truth here, that of Jesus' great love for sinners. No, the man did not put aside the weight and the desires that kept him from following the Lord, but that did not stop Jesus Himself from loving him! Beyond doubt, Jesus showed this man who rejected him such tender pity and compassion, seeing one struggling with a heart enslaved by sin and darkness. And that remains true today. Yes, Jesus feels a particular love for those who hear Him and follow Him. But let us not forget that the heart of Jesus has bottomless depths and is expansively wide in compassion and concern for those trapped in sin and faithlessness!"

Standing to his full height, the bishop finished with a flourish. "Men, there are among you today those who would beg off and wish to wander from Jesus. I say to you, He loves you more than your desire to turn away from Him. And there are those of you," and here Bishop John looked directly and tenderly at Jimmy, "who will say 'You do not understand, bishop. I am beyond help. I would not know where to begin. I know myself. I am the worst sort of man.' I tell you that the worst sort of man is exactly whom Jesus came to save. You may love the darkness of evil more than the light of Christ, but salvation is for the worst of men, if you will only heed your ignorance, see His great love, and throw yourself upon the grace and mercy of Jesus Himself!" He bowed his head, "Oh Lord Christ, move among those here today, even if only one man is clipped at his heart and moved into Your loving embrace, cause it to be so. We pray in Your blessed name, Amen!"

Even before Bishop John said *Amen*, Jimmy was out of his seat and moving toward him, the tears warm against his cheeks.

"I appreciate you joining me for the walk back to the factory," Jimmy said gratefully as he and John made the turn onto Langham Street.

"Think nothing of it, Jimmy," said John, "and I think my presence with you can assure your supervisor that everything is above board for your tardiness back to the afternoon shift."

"I also want to thank you for taking the time in another respect, Bishop," Jimmy replied.

"Call me John, please."

"Well ... John. I can truly say that until today, I never knew that I needed to turn away from my sin. And the more you spoke about the man in Mark's story, the more I thought I was the worst of sinners. But you showed me that is not the end."

"The worst of sinners, Jimmy," John said, grinning from ear to ear, "are all that Jesus has to save. He loves you, He rescued you, and now He desires to keep changing you because He loves you so dearly. And I would love to be a part of helping you grow in your new faith."

"I see that now," Jimmy said as they approached the iron gate of the factory. "It's strange. I left this factory this morning for a simple meal, and I am returning as a follower of Jesus Christ. This has been quite a new day."

John shook his hand heartily. "You went for a meal of ordinary food, and you happened to be fed with the Word of God. God knew what you needed. And I am grateful and humbled to have been part of that feast."

The Anglican minister **JOHN CHARLES RYLE** (1816-1900), more commonly known as J.C. Ryle, was one of the outstanding churchmen of the latter nineteenth century. Upon graduating from university, Ryle desired to stand for Parliament, but could not do so due to his father's financial ruin. This turned out to be a work of God's providence, as Ryle then studied for the ministry and ended up serving as rector for various congregations, faithfully preaching the Word of God in many towns and cities, including Norwich, Oxford, and Cambridge. In 1880, he was named the first bishop of Liverpool and served in that capacity until his death. His passionate evangelical spirit was evidenced in his clear, direct preaching and writing. Several of his books continue to be revered by readers today, including *Knots Untied,* his classic *Holiness,* and the highly readable *Expository Thoughts on the Gospels.* To his dying day, Ryle always sought to give hope to others by directing their hearts to the crucified Savior, Jesus Christ.

FACT FILES

The Church's Great Orators

From its beginning, the Church has been a growing family, one to whom God has communicated His Word so that gifted individuals might explain and apply those Scriptures to the lives of the followers of Jesus. This occurs in Christian worship in a number of ways. In singing, readings, the sacraments, and even the call to worship and benedictions, we come face to face with Scripture and can find it applicable to life. However, the primary and most obvious place is through biblical preaching. In the New Testament, we find the preaching of God's Word given primary status as God's people gather together. In Acts 2, new Christians met for worship and "devoted themselves to the apostles' teaching." In 2 Timothy 4, the apostle Paul urges his protégé Timothy to "[p]reach the Word; be ready in season and out of season." The preaching of Scripture in the Church is not optional, but rather the clear desire of God.

There have been many gifted Christian preachers down through the centuries, and we have already encountered some of them in previous volumes. John Chrysostom, Peter Waldo, John Wycliffe, John Calvin, John Knox, George Whitefield, and Charles Spurgeon are a few of the many great pulpit[1] orators down through history. Since the dawn of the twentieth century, there have been a number of preachers who have left their marks in Christian memory, as well.

In the history of the American people, it is impossible to adequately tell the story of ethnic justice without the impact of **Dr. Martin Luther King** (1929-1968). Although King never reached forty years of age, his impact on the

1. A pulpit is the place in the church where a minister preaches the sermon.

civil rights movement in the United States is far-reaching. A gifted speaker, King was able to utilize events from Scripture and draw parallels between those who endured injustice then and the African-American passion for equal rights. At a time when race relations in America were especially combustible, King's emphasis on nonviolent protests and his memorable preaching stirred the hearts of people across ethnic lines. In May 1956, King preached in New York City, his sermon entitled "The Death of Evil Upon the Seashore". Drawing upon the experience of the Hebrews in Exodus escaping from slavery in Egypt, King expressed hope and faith that God would also deliver African-Americans from their experienced oppressions. On August 28, 1963, at the Lincoln Memorial in the March on Washington, King gave perhaps his most iconic message, known as "I Have a Dream." Urging a vision for civil and economic rights and calling for an end to racism, King wove biblical allusions into the fabric of his message. When he expressed "I have a dream that every valley shall be exalted", he was connecting present hope to the words of Isaiah 40:4-5. As he declared that "justice rolls down like waters, and righteousness like an ever-flowing stream", he was quoting from the prophet Amos.[2] Even to the end of his life, King kept his sermons full of connections to Scripture. The night before he was tragically assassinated in Memphis, Tennessee, King spoke to a congregation and declared, like the prophet Moses, "I have been to the mountaintop ... And I've looked over. And I've seen the promised land. I may not get there with you. But I want you to know tonight, that we, as a people, will get to the promised land."

From a very different environment, the Welsh preacher *David Martyn Lloyd-Jones* (1899-1981) originally trained to be a physician. In fact, he assisted Sir Thomas Horder, who

---

2. Amos 5:24, to be exact.

was the primary doctor for several British monarchs and prime ministers, and Lloyd-Jones even became a member of the Royal College of Physicians! He was afflicted with restlessness, however, because he kept sensing God had called him to preach the Scriptures. After a short time of ministry near Port Talbot in his native Wales, in the year 1939, Lloyd-Jones was asked to come to Westminster Chapel in London, to serve as an associate pastor under G. Campbell Morgan. The prolific Morgan retired four years later, and Lloyd-Jones succeeded him as the senior pastor there.

Throughout his ministry at Westminster Chapel over the next twenty-five years, Lloyd-Jones emphasized the expository preaching of the Bible. In his book *Preaching and Preachers*, he defined preaching as "logic on fire". In other words, the preacher must use careful thought and preparation but ultimately the Holy Spirit brings the teaching of Scripture alive in the communication of the message. Lloyd-Jones believed a preacher was called by God to clarify and broaden the primary meaning of the text being explored in the sermon, connect it elsewhere in Scripture, and show how the teaching was both essential and practical for the listener. Lloyd-Jones was hardly a dry figure in the pulpit; his careful preparation of sermons was followed by a passionate delivery when he preached. Many of his teachings on Scripture made their way into books and commentaries, such as his lengthy series on the *Epistle to the Romans*, as well as other classic works like *Spiritual Depression* and *Authentic Christianity*.

The African-American Baptist preacher **E.K. Bailey** (1945-2003) might have inhabited a different landscape from Martyn Lloyd-Jones, but both men strongly believed in the surpassing value of expository preaching of the Bible. Bailey came from a long line of preachers, as his father, brother, uncles, and godfather were all ministers.

After his own theological training in north Texas, Bailey served at a church for six years before sensing that God was leading him to launch a new endeavor. In 1975, Bailey and two hundred others established Concord Missionary Baptist Church in Dallas, where he would remain as pastor over the remaining twenty-eight years of his life.

It was at Concord Church that Bailey wedded together two worlds of preaching. At the center of the African-American church experience was narrative preaching, where the preacher would not give the main idea at the start of the sermon, but through stories and illustrations he would lead the congregation to the big idea in an imaginative manner. Bailey believed in the power of illustrations to give people greater understanding of what biblical truth was, but he also trusted that the preacher's task must be expository. Such preaching, he said, focused on Scripture, determined the precise meaning of a passage, and led the hearers to adopt the direction of the passage so the Holy Spirit could transform their lives. By this expository approach joined with a high view of imaginative reinforcement, Bailey was able to inspire other preachers, as well. In 1995, Concord Church launched the annual E.K. Bailey Preaching Conference, which brought preachers from a variety of denominational and socio-ethnic backgrounds to model expository preaching through proclamation and various workshops, speaking to both the head and the heart.

The pastor and professor **Haddon Robinson** (1931-2017) also made great contributions to the Church during his life. Not just content to preach in churches, Robinson committed himself to teaching others how to communicate the Scriptures clearly. He taught homiletics (the study and skill-development of preaching) at Denver Seminary and Gordon-Conwell Seminary for many years, preparing many students for a lifetime of work in understanding and proclaiming the Bible with authority and passion. Robinson was a champion of what was called "the Big Idea" of preaching. He believed a sermon should be about one major idea, even if it could be subdivided into several parts. Keeping the sermon focused on one idea enabled listeners to better understand the clear teaching of the text. Like E.K. Bailey and Martyn Lloyd-Jones, Robinson believed preaching should be expository and be rooted in the Scripture, because that method takes the Bible seriously and allows the Scriptures to be the authority for the sermon, not the preacher. Toward the end of his life, Robinson also desired to connect biblical preaching and teaching to the everyday experience of ordinary Christians, so he helped found the Theology of Work Project, which continues to this day.

Back across the Atlantic Ocean, in the heart of London's bustling activity, **John Stott** (1921-2011) brought the vibrancy of the Gospel to life through careful, direct preaching. Stott was a productive churchman and faithful minister, serving as the rector at All Souls' Church, Langham Place in London where he had trusted in Christ years before, following a sermon on Revelation 3:20 ("Behold, I stand at the door and knock"). Stott was gripped by the hope that Jesus offered him that day and placed his faith in Christ as a result. Believing that Scripture was essential for the growth of Jesus' followers, Stott committed himself to careful study of the Bible, explaining passages vividly from the pulpit and giving clear application to the lives of believers. He also wrote *Between Two Worlds,* his classic book on preaching in which he sets forth his passion: Total confidence in God's Word in preaching will bring spiritual health to the Church and help believers grow and mature in Christ. So great was his desire for people to know Jesus that he let nothing stop him from proclaiming the Gospel. Once in Sydney, Australia, Stott lost his voice and was reduced to a hoarse whisper. Still, he rasped a message into a microphone at a university event there. He was not able to 'croak' much louder than that. And yet whenever he returned to Australia, someone always approached him and said, "Do you recall that time in the university's great hall when you lost your voice? I came to Christ that night."

One final great preacher worthy of mention is **J. Alec Motyer** (1924-2016). While Moyter is known for being a college principal and academic leader in England[3]— his commentaries on the Old Testament are clear, rich, and insightful—he was also known as a highly regarded preacher. He encountered the Bible at an early age, having listened to his grandmother in Ireland read biblical stories to him in compelling fashion. Motyer served as a vicar in an Anglican church and became known for several components of his preaching. He always believed that the goal of the preacher was to discover the big idea of a biblical text; in short, what is the one thing God wants to communicate in a passage. And then once the preacher has discovered that, what is the redemptive focus? By this, Motyer desired to communicate how we are to be transformed through Scripture: What does God reveal about Himself? Is there a promise we must believe? What does this passage reflect back upon or reveal about Jesus and His work?

While Motyer was a teacher in the academic world, he desired to help make other ministers into competent and biblically faithful preachers. He wrote *Preaching?: Simple Teaching About Simply Preaching* to this effect. Most

---

3. One personal item about Motyer: He was also someone who had deep personal relationships with others and made them feel valued. My own father was a friend of Motyer while the latter was still alive. In 2015, Dad was over in England speaking at different churches and had the opportunity to stop at Motyer's home for a visit, which would turn out to be their last encounter before Motyer's death the next year. Motyer asked Dad about the entire Davis family, including myself, my brothers, our families, and how we were all doing. Motyer had a heart brimming over with kindness and love.

of all, Motyer believed that to proclaim God's Word well, one should love the Bible intensely. If God has desired to communicate Himself to us, we should treasure God's efforts and love His story! Motyer made this a central feature of his own life, saying that "I'm not really a scholar. I'm just a man who loves the Word of God."

The blood of Jesus Christ gives hope and redemption to His people, but as history goes on, the oxygen that the Church breathes comes from the faithful preaching of Scripture. By the grace of God, He still raises up and calls preachers to that noble task.

B.B. WARFIELD

October 1902, Princeton, New Jersey

The Princeton campus was awash in the vibrant yellows, oranges, and reds from the leaves that hung on to tree branches for dear life. The sun had just peeked through the clouds and bathed the lawns in its generous glow. Hungry students were scurrying about at the lunch hour, turning the initial trickle of souls into a stream of humanity going in search of midday nourishment. In the midst of the shuffling feet and hurried movements, a single figure moved eastward from the seminary buildings and took the path toward Witherspoon Hall on the university side, mentally rehearsing what needed to be done when he reached his home.

"Dr. Warfield!" a student called out. The walker looked back toward the seminary and saw one of his students raising his hand as if hailing a carriage for transport. "Dr. Warfield, I know we just finished in the lecture hall, but I do have a few questions to ask you, if you have the time."

Peering more closely, Warfield saw the figure approaching. "Ah, Gresham!" He stopped, allowing the student time to come alongside him. "I am heading home, but if you wish, we can walk and talk on the way and continue the conversation over lunch, if you wish."

"A lunch invitation?" Gresham replied. "I am most humbled. And as it turns out, I have no classes until mid-afternoon." He fell in step with his professor and they continued on the path across the university grounds.

"Oh, it will be standard lunch fare for our abode," Warfield smiled kindly. He made a left turn but looked back at the towering maple near Witherspoon Hall. "That is a most impressive spire of our Lord's creation, and all the more magnificent this time of the year." He looked at Gresham with a slight twinkle in his eye. "Reds, yellows, and oranges bring the world to life during autumn, don't you agree?"

"Our Creator certainly knows what He is doing," Gresham affirmed. "Are you sure I wouldn't be imposing my presence on you?"

"I invited you, Gresham," Warfield responded. "No imposition at all. If you would be so kind, I will need time to prepare the meal. Nothing grand, just chicken, hard cheese, and bread. We can talk in the main room while Annie joins us."

"Annie?"

"My wife," said Warfield, his voice husky with both pleasure and sadness. "You'll enjoy her company."

The cozy domicile, named Hodge House, was located just southwest of Alexander Hall and offered enough warmth from the chilly air that had invaded New Jersey over the previous night. Dr. Warfield was very competent if somewhat fussy over the procedure of laying out the meat, cheese, and bread on a larger platter for transport to the main room of the house. He had Gresham place a clean cloth on a small table before lowering the platter on it.

"Gresham, if you would be so good," Warfield said, wiping his hands, "could you bring three plates, three cloth napkins, and also the water pitcher from the kitchen? Just place them here on the table, and I will go and fetch Annie for lunch."

Agreeably, Gresham did as asked but kept a quizzical eye on the hallway toward the Warfield's bedroom. Since arriving as a student at the beginning of the term, he had heard rumors that Dr. Warfield never spent more than a couple of hours away from home any day. His classes had been so arranged to make this possible. Bringing the items back into the living area, he deposited them on the table and turned around to see Warfield leading a woman who was slightly stooped in posture and looked about with nervous, if friendly, eyes. To Gresham, she appeared to be at least sixty-five years of age, but knowing that Warfield himself was only about fifty, he realised she must actually be younger than her appearance. She brushed a strand of graying hair away from her eyes as Dr. Warfield gently helped her into an armchair and then straightened up.

"Gresham," he said, his voice thick with emotion, "I'd like you to meet my beautiful wife, Annie. Annie, this is Gresham Machen, one of my first-year students in Greek."

Gresham bowed slightly and held up his hand for a brief wave, unsure how to approach Annie, who suddenly said, "Summer birthday, Ben!"

Taken aback, Gresham asked, "Pardon?"

Dr. Warfield chuckled at the confused look on Gresham's face. "It's perfectly fine, Gresham. Annie must have recognized your name from the student list. We collect the birthdays for all seminary students and make sure they receive written notes on those days as we celebrate them. Annie is good about remembering birthdays, aren't you, dear?"

Annie smiled, dropping her eyes and placing a finger gently to her temple. "Some things I can remember and I feel quite proud."

"Well, you were correct, Mrs. Warfield," Gresham assured her. "July the twenty-eighth is my birthday. I'll be twenty-two years old then. I look forward to your note."

Placing a portion of chicken, two cuts of cheese, and a slice of bread on a plate, Warfield served his wife and sat down in a chair next to her, gesturing to Gresham to take the small sofa. "Annie, I invited Gresham here because he had questions about class, so I thought lunch would be a fine time for him to come and meet you as well. I imagine you have several questions, Gresham."

Swallowing a bite of chicken, Gresham wiped his mouth with a cloth. "Plenty, but I also would like to ask about you both. Have you lived here for some time?"

"Since we arrived at Princeton fifteen years ago," Warfield said, sipping some water. "Before that, I was a pastor in Baltimore and taught in Pittsburgh. And before that, we were married and then spent our honeymoon in Germany." He patted Annie's hand. "I was studying in Leipzig and we moved there for a brief time."

Gresham was going to reply, but he saw Annie's lips begin to quiver and tears splash from her eyes. Warfield closed his hand around her own and whispered, loud enough for Gresham to hear, "It will be fine, dearest. We needn't go on. I'll let Gresham ask his questions." Turning to Gresham, he said, "Perhaps you can pose your Greek queries now. It would be more proper for the moment."

After that, it was all principal parts of verbs and declensions and translation matters of the New Testament text for the next twenty minutes. Annie occasionally looked over at Gresham and her husband chatting away and always had a smile for them both. But Gresham could discern some pain in her visage, and it was with no small relief when someone knocked on the door and Warfield said, "Ah, Annie, that'll be Mrs. Billings to see to you."

Mrs. Billings was a stout woman who proved herself gentle in handling Annie and helping her across the room. As she was leaving, Annie said haltingly, "I'm sorry I am not better company, Mr. Machen. I look forward to seeing you again."

Gresham stood and nodded toward her as Dr. Warfield rose and approached his wife. "Rest, dear, and if you like, we can take a walk later and enjoy the trees."

"I should like that very much, dearest Ben," Annie replied, kissing her husband lightly on the lips. "The oaks and ashes are delightful this time of year." And with that, she shuffled out of the room with Mrs. Billings.

"I assume there is a story behind your wife's reaction to Leipzig?" Gresham asked Warfield when they were alone again. "And I gather it is not due to the German culture."

"You noticed all that from her facial expression," Warfield noted dryly, "and you are not wrong. It was something that had nothing to do with Germany, with my academic pursuits, or with being in a foreign country. It happened in the Alps as we were taking a stroll. We had gone away from Leipzig for a few weeks. We weren't in the higher elevations and were completing our walk when a thunderstorm smashed through our area and lightning struck nearby several times. Poor Annie. She crumpled to the ground like a frightened rabbit and stayed there as the storm overwhelmed us in all its fury. I held her and tried to shield her from the terror, but the shock of it all devastated my poor Annie. It meant that my new bride was so crushed by the fright of the moment that she has not truly recovered. We have been to more physicians than I can count, and even though we are able to take short walks around Princeton and she remembers my students, it also means the woman whom I married is markedly different. My dearest Annie is the one I adore; I also have to face each day that she is not the woman I married. And yet my Savior and Lord has seen fit to make me content with such circumstances."

"She still engages in conversation," Gresham replied, "and I am impressed by her recall of my birthday."

"Some things she retains," Warfield agreed, "but she tires very easily. Being able to take her for a walk around the grounds is a significant moment. She loves to see the trees ... "

Warfield paused to wipe his eyes, which had become moist with tears. "I am sorry. Annie has shared my love of science and nature and the beauty of God's creation for so long. It is one of the most treasured things that makes her radiate with joy. I don't know how much longer I have with her, so I believe I must fill her life with as much hope as I can. And that involves being present with her."

"This is why you are constantly heading in this direction at certain hours," Gresham blurted out. "Because of your devotion to your wife? I have heard from many that you had to step down as principal of the seminary due to that. I'm sorry if that sounds presumptuous."

"No, not due to Annie," Warfield cautioned him, "but I have wanted to focus on teaching more than being an administrator."

Warfield leaned back in his chair. He had grown used to new students showing surprise at his unique responsibilities, but he always loved to speak about why he lived as he did. "Gresham, let me ask you a question in reply. Why did you come to Princeton?"

"Me?" Gresham replied. "Because Princeton offers me a fine education. I love the life of the mind. I have an opportunity to gain degrees from both the university and the seminary at the same time. And God provided that I should do so."

"Good, good," Warfield agreed, "But let me ask you some additional questions. Why learn about Scripture? Why take theology classes? Why learn Greek from me?"

Gresham grew more cagey, sensing Warfield was leading him in an unseen direction. "Well, I would say to know the Bible. To be able to teach and preach the Bible. To understand God so I might help others understand Him. And to know the original languages so I might know what the Bible says."

Warfield smiled. He carefully folded the napkin that was in his hand and placed it on the lunch tray before standing. "Let us go, Gresham. We'll talk further on the way back, for you have a class and so do I."

After Dr. Warfield kissed Annie goodbye they took a different path on their return. Skirting the west side of Blair Hall, they could view the seminary buildings across the street. Their time had been spent in such companionable silence that Gresham flinched when Warfield revived their conversation.

"You were right, you know," he said, "about what you said before, Gresham. And yet I would urge you to not let those be your only justifications for being here."

"Are you saying education is not beneficial in and of itself?" Gresham asked.

"Not that, not that," the professor responded. "I want you to know that your education will—it must—lead you to considerations outside of yourself, Gresham. You may become a great churchman one day and call others to faithfulness to Jesus Christ. But to do so, you must cast your view outside the academy and toward the care of others and love them well. Do not live away from, but live within the midst of others, their hopes, their fears, and their tears. Wherever people suffer, be there to comfort them as the Holy Spirit comforts you in your affliction. Wherever others strive and seek, be there to give them strength as our Father God gives us strength. Whenever others fail, be there to lift them up, remembering that our Lord Jesus Himself graciously died to lift us from sin and wickedness into His embrace."

Gresham was speechless. He had no response, but he knew instinctively his teacher was right. Warfield went on, his hand on Gresham's shoulder as they walked.

"Above all, Gresham, God requires you forget yourself in others. You must not live a solitary life, but many lives, bonded to others in their sadness and smiles, their tears and triumphs. God is making you fit to live with Him forever. To do that, He desires you to live as a godly and compassionate shepherd to those on earth."

Their steps slowed as they approached the seminary building when Gresham remarked, "You have given me more food for thought than I imagined I would receive today, Dr. Warfield. I cannot thank you enough."

"I receive that," Warfield replied, "from the hand of God who has given me a wonderful wife. Every time I behold her, I am reminded of my own frailty and weakness before my Lord." His tears began to flow. "And that means my dearest Annie helps me live the Gospel each day. Because of that, I love my Lord Jesus even more. And because of Christ, I love my sweet Annie more and more."

The theologian **BENJAMIN BRECKINRIDGE WARFIELD** (1851-1921) was the last of the great "Princeton Theologians" of the late nineteenth and early twentieth centuries. Originally studying mathematics and science, he studied theology and became a Presbyterian pastor and renowned professor at Princeton Seminary from 1887 to his death. He was known for his clear teaching on the authority and trustworthiness of the Bible, salvation in Christ, and his warm and personal relationships with his students. He wrote a number of books and influenced countless students over his years at Princeton, but his greatest legacy was his durable faithfulness in the midst of many challenges. Most of all, Warfield displayed deep affection and care for his wife Annie in her disability and limitations, never leaving her for more than two hours at a time and always showing Christ-like love for his bride.

FRANCIS GRIMKE

April 1918, Washington, D.C.

"Ahhh," exhaled the minister, the taller of the two black men ambling around Thomas Circle as they aimed for Vermont Avenue in a southwesterly direction. "Can you smell that, Stephen? I swear, this has to be the most glorious time of the year in this city. That breeze coming from the south bears that smell so wondrously I do believe the air is sweet enough to eat."

"You never fail as a wordsmith, Reverend Grimke," said his companion, adjusting his hat and then smoothing the front of his suit. "We just had lunch and you are making me hungry for a dessert by your description of the cherry blossoms."

Francis Grimke beamed at the compliment. "Then you'll be positively ravenous by the time we get to the Tidal Basin. I love beholding the blooms while they appear for just this short while." He looked around him as they passed an inn on their right and continued on toward K Street, shifting his Bible from his right hand to his left. "Walking does help one digest a meal, but it would be more conducive to our feet if we could hail a coach and manage to ride to the blossoms."

"It's just a mile away as the crow flies," offered Stephen, breathing more heavily than his pastor, "but I wouldn't mind more efficient means of travel. We have choir practice tonight at the church and I will take any chance to save my lungs. But do you think someone will be willing to give us a ride?" He held up his hands. "All things considered with our skin color?"

"Our nation's original sin is a stain, for sure," Francis replied, "but you must give others the opportunity to repent and see the light of our freedom more clearly. Some of us have spent more time in that light than others, and for others our liberty seems to be a sudden thing. All we can do is tell the truth plainly, directly, with hope. And maybe that begins with a coach driver willing to take us to the Tidal Basin. Maybe it doesn't. But like with all things, we will get there."

Stephen looked ahead as they approached K Street. It wasn't unusual for several people to be milling about in McPherson Park, he thought, but there was a considerable amount of unrest in the movements of the people he could see. "Reverend," he said, pointing forward, "d'you think there's trouble ahead?"

Francis strained his eyes, knowing his glasses were not helping him see at far distances as he would like. "That's more people than usual in the park this time of day," he muttered, "and that's a mixed crowd." He quickened his pace. "Might need to get there and quell whatever it is going on." Lengthening his stride and waving Stephen on to do the same, he sighed, "Trouble's a-brewing!"

The two men arrived in the center of McPherson Park moments later as shouts and screams rent the air. Francis looked past the angry gathering to the White House, situated only a quarter mile away. The crowd's shrill volley had only grown louder and it was clear their attention was focused on a fight at the center of that mass of humanity. Francis and Stephen pushed aside several onlookers and stumbled into two teenage boys throwing punches at each other! Within seconds, Francis grabbed the arms of the slightly heavier boy and pinned them to his side. Stephen tackled the other and held him to the ground. As if disappointed by the interruption, the bystanders carped and called.

"Aye, ya shoulda let them go at it till he clocked him clean!" called out one man behind Francis. The pastor looked down at the young man in his arms and saw he was a well-tanned athletic type who was no doubt Caucasian. Looking over at Stephen, Francis saw his friend was restraining a teen whose skin was as dark as his own.

Lord Jesus, Francis prayed silently, *help me. Show us how we can bring peace.*

"Let me go!" said the white boy, kicking backward against Francis' shins. "You don't know what brought this on, so let me go!"

Sensing the crowd's frustration with him, Francis tightened his grip around the boy's body and put his mouth next to his ear. "I will release you, young man, but your fight time is officially over!" He let go, the boy spinning away from him and ending up on the ground in a clumsy fall. Springing to his feet and dusting himself off, he glared at Francis and shouted.

"Keep your hands off me, you ... " and unleashed a vile slur against the pastor. Francis recoiled at the force of the epithet. In an instant, he imagined himself back at school in his South Carolina days, receiving an education with his free Black friends but listening to the abuse hurled at them in the streets by the bigoted tongues of their white counterparts.

"You ain't gonna say that to the reverend!" shouted Stephen, so eager to defend Francis that he accidentally let go of his charge, who bounded up to re-start the fight. However, Francis interposed his lanky frame and stuck his right palm in the lad's chest, whirling around and keeping the other boy at bay with the thick Bible in his left hand.

"What in the world has gotten into you two?" Francis thundered above the groans of the crowd who desired an extension of the fight. Looking around, he saw the reason for their disappointment: Out of the sixty adults there, at least fifty were white, while the ten or so Black men were on the periphery, wearing determined faces although clearly outnumbered. *Lord Jesus, I'm asking you, help me!* Francis prayed.

"He started it!' said the Black youth whom Stephen had tackled.

"Over what?" Francis inquired loudly, trying to cool the tension. "Is it because of the New York ball cap he's wearing and you're sticking up for the Senators?"

"Let 'em fight," said a stocky, blond-haired man behind Francis. "It's none of your business what they do. Just let 'em go!"

"Because of what?" roared Francis to the crowd. "You all have the numbers by five to one and you say not to get involved?"

"Who are you to say that?" sneered another white man behind the blond one.

Before Francis could respond, one of the Black men on the south end of the crowd piped up. "I'll tell you who he is!" he railed. "That's Reverend Grimke. You're at the church on Fifteenth Street!"

"I am," Francis agreed, "and you can accept or refuse that I have the right to speak my mind, but any fight between two young men of this nature has no merit!" Pointing a finger in turn at each of the boys, he barked, "Now what is the source of your disagreement?"

"It sure ain't baseball!" said the white youth.

"It's what he called me!" shouted the other. "The same thing he called you, Reverend!"

Francis looked back at the teen, who looked about to respond harshly, but upon seeing the pastor's eyes, he recoiled and looked down.

"This true?" Francis asked.

"It is. That's what I said. No denying it," he mumbled, adjusting his Yankees cap.

"Yank," Francis said, hoping the use of the team's name would give him some collateral with the boy, "what are you doing by saying that?"

"He may have said it to the boy and to you, but how often do you get called that anyway?" said the blond man again to the murmurs of the crowd. "You aren't exactly as dark as coal, and I don't think that's the sun throwing me off!"

The people grew silent after that accusation. They hardly expected the pastor's reaction, though. Turning from the boys and facing his adversary, Francis softened his gaze and his voice.

"That's where you are mistaken about what I have been called before." Francis replied in a quiet yet powerful tone. "You have no idea about my life, so that's exactly where you're wrong."

Noting the black youth trying to sneak off, Francis turned and called to him. "And you! Why did you think that settling things with your fists was the better choice? You get called that, and your first inclination is to fight? Please tell me why!"

"It's more than that," was the reply. "Kid's carping on about the war and how America's gonna win and make the world safe for everyone. Well, my uncle's over in France fighting in the war and he gets treated no better by the army there than here! He and the others get put to work in the kitchens, transport, everything but going to the front. It's like the white officers don't think they're good enough fighters!"

"You're just slinging lies!" chirped his counterpart.

"92nd Division, he is," the other exploded, his dark hands balling into fists. "You can believe what you want, but trust me, the truth will come out!"

"This is enough!" Francis ordered, with a glint in his eye. "If you won't listen to each other, then listen to me!"

"What you got to say, preacher man?" chortled someone near the back, his voice betraying a Virginia accent.

"I have plenty to say, so you'll have plenty to listen to," Francis demanded. His voice was calm but steady. Something in it quieted the crowd, as if they recognized his authority.

Francis cleared his throat and spoke. "I have lived for many years here in this city, but I am no native of this territory! Though I've been on the Lord's earth for sixty-seven years, I was born in the heat of South Carolina before the war that tore our nation apart. Many of you might well look down upon me for the color of my skin, while others," he pointed at the minority, "might believe my skin is not dark enough. That is because I am the product of a union between white and black, slave owner and slave woman. And that is where I first came to know this amalgamation of slavery's evil mixed with my owner's provision. There I was taught to read, to write, to be productive, and yes—you see that gifts still in use today were granted me in the darkness of servitude. When the master died, he wished my mother and brothers be treated as family, but that did not stop his brother from claiming us as his slaves. And I had to make a choice—live in the darkness or risk the run to the light. I thought I could avoid the former without doing the latter, so I joined the Confederates so I could avoid slavery. I was a valet in a jail housing Northern soldiers. But returned to my master, I had to make the choice again—live in the darkness or run to the light. And I ran away. I hid with my family rather than live in slavery. Because that is what God calls us to do, to hide in his hands rather than serve a false master in Satan!"

"Is that why you wave your Bible here, preacher?" another called out, but without the bravado of the others.

"If one stands here in this city and holds up the Word of God, he must call people to the God of that Word and not use Scripture in any other way!" Francis said in a voice that grew more melodious with each passing sentence. "The Word of God that calls us to freedom acknowledges the sinfulness of mankind. God himself shows in his Word that in seeking his dream for the flourishing of his people, we must prepare to confront evil! And that truth sustained me in the segregated schooling I received in Charleston! And the Spirit of the Lord sustained me as I received money for college in Pennsylvania, but no funding for books or clothes, and yet God made a way. God made a way that I might proclaim the excellencies of his Son, Jesus Christ, who is the way, the truth, and the life. And that Jesus who responded in love and grace when others demeaned him, hated him, and killed him ... that Jesus led me on to be trained to preach the Word of God, to proclaim Christ and him crucified!"

A spell had come over the crowd. Even the two youths who had been scrapping minutes before exchanged knowing glances and nodded in agreement. Stephen was breathless with amazement.

"That is my story, O people," he continued. "But I do not believe my friend and I did come here by accident today. No, God has brought us here because our story must align with your own. Does bigotry exist in this nation? Does prejudice erupt on the battlefields of Europe today? Yes, but it need not be so! And that is why I do believe this moment is of divine appointment. We all stand here within sight of the White House, which bears its own guilt by its role in evicting so many of my Black brothers from positions of influence in our government. To all of you today, I say this: Do not place your hope in government, in political parties, or even your own hearts which are so riven by sin. Jesus has brought us together today. You listen to him! Place your faith and trust in the Son of God and Savior of sinners, all of you! For many, that means being transformed by Christ in such a way that he conquers your prejudices and stamps out the bigotry clinging to your souls. It means breaking down the walls of separation you have erected. Commit to live your lives by God's standards and not others. Live in holiness of heart rather than comfort of body. Love your fellow man, see to his well-being, and defend him at all costs!"

Murmurs of agreement and not a few "amens" rippled through the crowd. Francis went on. "And you who are the targets of mistreatment and bigotry: This is upon your shoulders as well. When these men offer themselves to you, confessing their part in our nation's great original sin, will you refuse to forgive them? No, you will not. *Forgive us our debts,* we pray to our Heavenly Father, *as we forgive our debtors.* That is our obligation, my friends, no matter the color of your skin today. For one day, God's people from every tribe, tongue, and nation will worship him in heaven. I say we start living like it on earth!"

The passion of those words electrified those gathered, and in a moment that surprised even Francis himself, they clapped and cheered him like it was a political rally. Some approached others and offered apologies for words spoken and sentiments betrayed. Francis felt a tap on his arm and saw the two boys who had been fighting when he and Stephen had arrived.

"You're not leaving just yet, are you?" they asked.

Francis grinned broadly. "Brother Stephen and I were headed to the Tidal Basin to see the cherry blossoms, if you'd like to join us. We'd be glad of the company as long as you don't mind the walk."

"No need for that," said the blond man who had accosted Francis earlier on, a kind smile on his face now. "I can take you myself. My horse and coach are right over there."

Chuckling heartily and shaking the man's hand, Grimke looked at Stephen, who shook his head and marveled, "Divine appointment indeed!"

The African-American pastor **FRANCIS GRIMKE** survived slavery in the American South and graduated from Princeton Theological Seminary in 1878. One of the great Presbyterian preachers bridging the nineteenth and twentieth centuries, Grimke pastored at the Fifteenth Street Presbyterian Church in Washington, D.C., for over fifty years. A highly educated man of great character and confidence, Grimke ably blended Reformation theology with a clear focus on the application of the gospel to the problem of slavery. His voice is an important one in American history, as he was able to articulate hope and reconciliation even though his life had been forged in great oppression. As he confronted great evil, he always prioritized preaching the Gospel, calling people to repentance in Christ, and urging them to embrace the transforming power of the Holy Spirit.

DIETRICH BONHOEFFER

January 1943, Berlin, Germany

The two men walked south on Fasanenstrasse, passing the Savoy Hotel to their right, crossing the Kantstrasse, and proceeding by the ruins of a synagogue. The younger of the two bundled his coat around his collar to stave off the swirling wind. There seemed to be no relief from Berlin's bitter cold, and this sudden shift to even worse freezing temperatures made Dietrich Bonhoeffer[1] debate the wisdom of going to this meeting.

"Come along!" beckoned Hans, Dietrich's brother-in-law, after another hundred yards. "One doesn't expect you to enjoy the cold but brace yourself up and labor through it."

"A walk to the church is not half as bad when the breeze is going the other direction," complained Dietrich. "Why do we have to go on such a roundabout journey?"

"Mind your voice," Hans said quietly but firmly as he thumbed leftward, and they made the turn and sauntered eastward on the Kurfürstendamm[2] under the gray skies.

---

1. This is a re-imagining of Bonhoeffer's recruitment to the work of Operation Spark. It's known that Bonhoeffer's brother-in-law Hans Dohnányi had made initial contact with members of the German military intelligence service, and then brought Bonhoeffer into that movement. Leaders in this group included Wilhelm Canaris and Henning von Trescow, who appear in this chapter. Although Canaris and von Trescow would have been known to Bonhoffer, he likely might not have met with them until the time arose for Operation Spark. Although this meeting would not have occurred exactly in this way and place, the events of this chapter capture the essence of Canaris' and von Trescow's request to Bonhoeffer, as well as the struggle Bonhoeffer himself felt in making this momentous decision.

2. The Kurfürstendamm, or Ku'damm for short, is a famous boulevard in Berlin, presently lined with fashionable shops, restaurants, hotels, and houses. It is part

"A roundabout journey is just the thing. If we are too direct with our travels from headquarters, then we are more easily tracked." They went on in silence for a while, Hans occasionally feigning interest in the wares shown in many shop windows. After they had gone a third of a mile, he hissed, not looking at Dietrich, "Let's go in separately, brother. I'll go ahead. You follow behind me after two minutes. I'll see you inside with them."

"What am I supposed to do to give you some space?" Dietrich asked.

Rolling his eyes, Hans replied, "You figure it out! Look in a chocolate shop, see about a new necktie, whatever. We arrive separately, we look less suspicious. Honestly, Dieter," he huffed, using the shortened form of Dietrich's name, "if they could hear everything you let out of your mouth, we'd be arrested by now! Two minutes." And Hans quickened his pace and went ahead.

Slowing down and sitting on a bench, Dietrich untied his shoe, removed it, and shook it as if to unleash a troublesome pebble. In truth there was no pebble, but the day seemed troublesome all the same. *Why was I so willing to come along with Hans,* Dietrich asked himself. *And what is going to happen when I get there?*

The Kaiser Wilhelm Memorial Church[3] stood out like a giant index finger pointed defiantly toward heaven. Dietrich took the steps two at a time, rebuking himself for his quickness, but since he was at the door, there was nothing he could do.

The darkness of the church's interior was a change from the outdoor environment, and it took Dietrich some

---

of the central district of western Berlin and was named for the Kurfürsten, or prince-electors of the historic region of Brandenburg.

3. The Kaiser Wilhelm Memorial Church—originally built in the 1890s—was named after Kaiser Wilhelm I by his grandson, Wilhelm II, who was emperor of Germany until the end of the First World War in 1918. In November 1943, the church suffered catastrophic damage when bombed in an Allied air raid of Berlin.

time before he could see Hans up near the right transept[4], speaking in low tones with another two individuals. Two church wardens stood near the back pews, shuffling papers and organizing hymn books. It struck Dietrich that these "wardens" might have nothing to do with the church and have everything to do with looking out for trouble. He walked up the aisle and raised his hand to Hans, who nodded and cleared his throat to announce Dietrich's arrival, and the two others turned in the pew.

"Herr Bonhoeffer," said the one, his blond locks swept across his head complete with streaks of gray, betraying his fifty-six years of age.

The other, his posture as angular and military as the first one, was mostly bald with a touch of darker hair, but he appeared a good ten to fifteen years younger. "Ah, so this is the one who has come so highly recommended. Reverend Bonhoeffer, it is good to see you outside the military administrative walls."

"I don't know if introductions need to be made ... " began Hans, but Dietrich interrupted.

"None needed," he said. "I know of you both, and may I say, I am humbled by your confidence." He shook their hands in turn. "Admiral Canaris," he said to the first. To the second, he nodded, "Generalmajor[5] von Tresckow." Standing, he smoothed his suit lapels and asked, "I imagine this is important if we are to meet in a church." Inwardly, his heart nearly stopped. *These are two of the top members of the military seeking to overthrow Adolf Hitler,* he thought. *Meeting them here is well beyond 'important'. Something monumental is happening.*

"Important as in critical, secret, and as short as possible," said Admiral Wilhelm Canaris. "We need to move with all

---

4. In churches with a cruciform (cross-shaped) floor plan, the transepts are the two side areas, part of the crossing that divides the main church from the altar, choir, and pulpit. Think of a small letter "t" on its side to the right; the short line that crosses the "t" would be the transepts.

5. Von Tresckow's rank was major general, which in the German army was "generalmajor".

speed in our discussion, lest there be trouble. That is why we brought our bodyguards along."

"You mean the supposed church wardens in the back?" asked Dietrich.

"Those are staffers," remarked von Tresckow. "Our bodyguards are in the pastor's study keeping him at bay."

"The pastor?" Dietrich asked coldly.

Canaris stood up. "We have some lingering doubts about how 'sound' he is toward our goals." He gestured toward the wall behind them. "Perhaps you and I could walk a bit and take a look at the mosaics?" He relaxed his shoulders as they walked but it was not enough to disguise his military carriage. He pretended to admire a fresco of Christ on his throne as he said, "Herr Bonhoeffer, the *generalmajor* and I have a request for you. It is one that Hans is assisting in, and one in which we would require your help. We do not expect you to take our request lightly, but it is one that—as a member of the resistance within the Abwehr[6]—we would expect your heartfelt assistance." Canaris lifted his hand as if to ward off an expected protest from Dietrich. "I know, you have given invaluable effort so far. Your work as a courier and liaison to Allied governments has given us contacts with them that might well bear fruit. I've heard your meeting with Bishop Bell in Chichester was productive and that we might receive assistance from the British.[7]"

"We will see if those requests are successful," Dietrich allowed.

---

6. The *Abwehr* was the German military intelligence division. Begun in 1920, it continued through the entire time Nazi Germany was in power from 1933 to 1945. A number of ranking members of the Abwehr became participants in the resistance against Adolf Hitler and the Nazis, working to topple the regime from the inside.

7. George Bell, the bishop mentioned here, did indeed meet with Bonhoeffer and passed along a request to the British Foreign Office to help the German resistance and revolt against the Nazis. However, the British government ignored these pleas for help.

"In the meantime, though, we need you in another effort which takes you beyond liaison," Canaris continued. "We know we cannot expect every Allied nation to see things as clearly as we do. Of course, Britain, the United States, and others ... they would likely smell a trap that doesn't exist, and naturally, I can't blame them for a strong desire for self-preservation. That is why we must act quickly." They had circled back around in the sanctuary and were approaching the altar where von Tresckow appeared. "Hans is already deeply involved, and the generalmajor is the center of the day-to-day planning, but we believe there is strength in numbers, and we would urge your partnership in this endeavor."

The stocky von Tresckow brought a firm hand down on Dietrich's shoulder. "We have already put in motion a calculated risk; it might seem a gamble to some but we believe it is a necessary gamble. Very succinctly, we cannot wait for others to kill the snake, so we have to cut off his head ourselves. We have spent time planning it long enough. Now, we are ready. The spark[8] can now be set off."

"The spark?" asked Dietrich.

"In several weeks," said von Tresckow, "I will be in Russian territory. Smolensk, to be exact. Around that time, Hitler will be visiting the Army Group Centre there. We already have plans in place that when he does visit, he will be killed."

The enormity of what von Tresckow said staggered Dietrich like a boxer's punch. Sweat peppered his brow. "You speak of assassination, *generalmajor*," he exhaled.

"We speak of liberation of Germany from the Nazis' evil grip, the deliverance of Jews from extermination, and

---

8. Von Tresckow chose the third of the three options for Hitler's killing—having a timebomb smuggled in a case aboard Hitler's plane before the Führer departed and then time-delay detonated about a half-hour later. In the frigid temperature of the luggage hold, the percussion cap of the bomb became too cold and the bomb did not explode.

hope for the future," von Tresckow grunted, looking back over his shoulder. "Surely you wish all that."

"Of course I do!" Dietrich replied bluntly. "But you are speaking of taking the life of another, planned in advance, for a specific reason, through a specific way, at a specific time. Please explain to me how that is not murder."

"It's the Führer! Hitler himself!" growled Hans, who moved alongside his brother-in-law. "Surely you would believe that is reason enough, to bring down a monster of this nature, the enemy of civilization itself, and the mass murderer of millions! Can you not see that eliminating one evil man would mean the preservation of so many?"

Dietrich wiped his brow, his chest hurting from the tension in his body. He had confronted the evil of the Nazis time and again during his work with the Abwehr. Now he was being asked to participate at a much deeper level. Before he could answer, Canaris spoke.

"My dear Herr Bonhoeffer," the admiral spoke, keeping his voice low, "I know this is difficult for you. But might I remind you that some time ago, you proclaimed that people should be ready to act in the face of such evil."

"How do you know that?" Dietrich replied, unbelieving.

Canaris cracked his knuckles and looked up at the stained glass above the altar area. "Well before you were barred from preaching or writing, someone took detailed notes on one of your sermons some ten years ago. He shared those recollections with me and now I offer your words back to you." He stood at his full height. "You said, 'The blood of martyrs might once again be demanded'. Is that true?"

Dietrich could not deny it. "Yes, I said those words. The year before Hitler came to power. I had no idea they would take on such meaning now. But if we go down this path, it comes at a high price. Because I also followed those words about martyrdom by saying that if we possess courage to shed such blood, it will not be done innocently, like the apostles' deaths. We must be prepared to bear heavy guilt for our actions."

"And what is the greater guilt, sir?" asked von Tresckow. "The killing of one evil monster or to allow the many innocents to suffer at his hands?" The soldier gripped his riding crop so tightly Dietrich worried he might bring it down in fury on the altar itself.

Hans stepped up next to him and touched his arm. "You speak of this decision as if it is costly, my brother. Of course it is! But I think you've faced up to that before, haven't you?"

Why, oh why, thought Dietrich, *are they using my past writings in this way, O Lord? Do I really have the stomach for this?*

Looking in turn at the three men, Dietrich shrugged his shoulders. "I will admit that I have watched my fellow citizens passively watch as Hitler has executed his diabolical schemes. Even the large number of churches have given hearty approval to his vision of racial supremacy and evil. On Sunday, their ministers preach grace as an inexhaustible treasury, but one that never touches the human heart. All I hear is the siren song of cheap grace, of people assenting to their sins forgiven so their failings are justified. The vice-grip of Hitler over our country is due in large part to our own wallowing in the pigpen of cheap grace, and I cannot bear that. Too long I have seen forgiveness without requiring repentance, baptism without discipline, Communion without confession, and cleansing without the Cross! Oh, the way is necessary! Oh, the way is fraught with danger and overwhelming sorrow!"

Canaris looked at him and then the others before turning his gaze back to Dietrich. "Herr Bonhoeffer, I am a military man. Grace does not have a place in my world. We are a brotherhood of orders and obedience, not forgiveness and freedom. But in spite of your words which are alien to me, I believe you rightly recognize that this thing called grace has called you to something sacrificial, not superficial."

Dietrich looked upon the Communion table. There among the materials stood a brass cross, about a foot high. *Can I really say no to this request, Lord?* he prayed silently. *Can I really speak of your Gospel that I must seek again and again, your gift that must be asked for, the door at which I must knock until my knuckles bleed ... without saying yes to this?*

He looked at Canaris, von Tresckow, and then Hans. The weight sat hard in his chest. "If there seems to be no other way ... " he trailed off.

"There isn't," von Tresckow said quietly, looking strangely sympathetic.

"Then there is the responsible thing," said Dietrich. "Not to pull myself heroically from this, but to seek that future generations might live and flourish. Very well. We may justify our actions by necessity, or we may act according to conscience. When I stand before Christ my King, I will merely ask for grace. He grants such grace, as it is. Costly because it cost Jesus his life, and grace because he gives the only true life."

Canaris smiled, relieved to get Dietrich's agreement. "Well, thank you, Herr Bonhoeffer. And relax. Perhaps you won't find yourself standing before God anytime soon."

"Given my agreement to this plot, I am prepared for such a meeting," Dietrich responded, offering his hand to the admiral, "for when Christ calls a man, he bids him to come and die."

The German pastor and theologian **DIETRICH BONHOEFFER** (1906-1945) spent his adult life speaking out against a watered-down faith in the German churches and the injustice and evil of the Nazi regime. His time in America at Union Seminary in New York led him to a church that took seriously the call to confronting racial injustice, and he returned to Germany for good to speak out on behalf of the Jews against the Nazi's Holocaust. His work in the German military intelligence provided networks for him as he became more involved in the resistance against Adolf Hitler and the Nazi horrors, which he saw as living out his faith convictions. Sadly, Bonhoeffer was linked with the Operation Spark plot to assassinate Hitler, and he was arrested and imprisoned with his brother-in-law Hans, first at Tegel Prison and then at Flossenbürg concentration camp. There, on April 9th, 1945, three days before Allied forces liberated the camp, Bonhoeffer was led to the gallows and was hanged to death.

CORRIE TEN BOOM

December 1944, Ravensbrück, Germany

Gray, thought the woman as she flexed her fingers through much pain. *Everything about this place is dreary and gray.* The snowflakes, white as they were as they flitted through the air, would eventually mix with the dirt and grime on the walkways, creating a dingy color. Corrie felt a pain shoot up her right calf as the officer barked at her from behind.

"*Sich beeilen!*[1]" came her raspy shout, and Corrie continued along, pushing the overloaded cart of wires, metal, and engine parts in the direction of the factory. She wanted to stop and take a rest; she could feel every day of her fifty-two years of life in the weariness of her bones and aches in her muscles. Yet to delay in any manner risked a torrent of abuse from the guard, a sturdy and tall lass who was known to use the butt of her rifle to torment a prisoner. The cruelty of the female guards like the one trailing Corrie—Ravensbrück was the only concentration camp to employ women in that role[2]—was well known throughout the barracks. Just last week, it was said, she had beaten two women so savagely they had been carried off to the infirmary and then never returned.

"*Ja, ja*[3]," Corrie replied sweetly, determined to keep moving and not risk a beating. She shuffled down the

---

1. This German expression means "Hurry up!" or "Move along!"
2. Ravensbrück was the largest concentration camp within Nazi Germany's prewar borders exclusively for women prisoners, and after Lichtenburg closed in 1939, it was the only main concentration camp almost exclusively for women.
3. German (and Dutch) for "yes, yes"

path, her muscles strained as she pushed the cart onward. And yet it was more than this physical strain she bore in the moment. So much weight fell on her heart, the pain of the past mixing with her present anxiety. Not wanting the guard to notice her sorrow or give it away by a slower pace, Corrie intentionally lengthened her stride as much as she could, finally turning the cart toward a door leading to a storage room at the factory. Depositing the load near the threshold, she looked beyond the walls toward the Schwedtsee[4], then turned to await further orders from the trailing guard. Steeling herself to expect anything—a clipped command, a sneer, even a brief beating for not being as speedy as expected—she was shocked to behold a nod of appreciation and a brief smile.

"Thank you," she said, waving Corrie back north toward the path leading toward the workshops. "I will see to it that these are collected. You are to go to the shop floor and cover another's shift."

Gulping in disappointment, Corrie managed to respond kindly, in German, "Yes. Still, I was hoping to visit my sick sister in the infirmary. I was promised time to do that."

The guard's face darkened, and she shook her head slowly but firmly. "No, you are to be elsewhere. Sergeant's orders." She pointed again toward the far door. "Now go. I do not wish to be harsh toward you, and your sister may be ill, but orders are orders."

Exhausted but determined to display a good work ethic, Corrie sat at the table in the shop, her pained and calloused fingers working a screwdriver that tightened plate after plate, connecting them to more toggle switches than she could count. The pain in her fingers was bad enough, but it was nothing compared to the pain in her heart regarding her sister's health.

4. The Schwedtsee is a lake that sits on the west side of where Ravensbrück stood.

Apparently, Corrie was not hiding her anxiety well from her fellow prisoners. Looking up at the woman across the table from her, Corrie saw her companion looked deeply concerned. She took a deep breath and mouthed, "Sorry, I am not myself."

"With all you have been through," the woman whispered back, "I think that can be forgiven. You just looked as if you were recovering from the spinner."

"Spinner?" Corrie asked, keeping her voice extremely low. The guards were monitoring the activity in the shop, but Ravensbrück women had developed a keen ability to hold conversations at minimal volume, beyond the earshot of their superiors.

"It is a game my people play, the spinner," she replied, "where children stand where they are, hold out their arms, and spin around for several moments. Once the spinning stops, the children try to stand as long as possible. The spinning makes one so dizzy that children end up falling down, and the final person standing wins."

"Your people?" Corrie inquired.

"My people," her companion responded. "Yes, I am Romani.[5] My name is Eldorai ... something like Hildegard." She brushed a strand of hair away from her dark face. "I was going to say that it is an honor to sit with you at last."

"An honor?" Corrie whispered even more slightly than before, as a guard walked by their table.

Waiting until it was safer, Eldorai nodded as she connected a switch box together. "An honor, yes," she said, her voice cotton-soft. "I have enjoyed your studies and prayers. I am in the bunk at the opposite end of the cellhouse from you, and when you and Betsie have led

5. The Romani, sometimes called Gypsy, are a people group scattered throughout Europe and the world, with a distinct culture and tradition. Because the Nazis did not view the Romani as pure-blooded Germans, they were persecuted and targeted cruelly as "enemies of the Aryan state", receiving the same designation as the Jews. Somewhere between a quarter-million to a half-million Romani perished under the Nazi regime.

worship, I tend to be farthest away in the gathered group. But I have listened. And I have prayed. And last month, I received your Jesus and prayed that I might follow him. Thanks be to Jesus and to His Word, that Bible that you both had smuggled into the camp!"

"Every time I start to lose heart about being here," Corrie smiled, "I remember God has His purpose! And to hear your words gives me such joy!"

"I do not know why you are even here," Eldorai murmured, "for you are not Romani nor Jew nor Jehovah's Witness. I have not heard the story of your arrival."

"Because we were harboring Jews in our house," Corrie said after a long pause and grimacing as she screwed on yet another toggle switch plate. "We had a small nook in our home in Haarlem—I'm from Holland—above our watch shop. My father had begun to take in Jews who needed safety. The Gestapo[6] were rounding up Jews, and we knew what their fate would be if caught. So we began taking in a few at a time, hiding them in that small place in our home, barely larger than a closet, until they could escape. It was behind a false wall in my bedroom, well ventilated, and we could use a buzzer to warn them to hide there if officers came by."

"That sounds dangerous!"

"Yes, but my father Casper believed that if we are to follow Christ, we must be willing to give up our comforts and save others who are powerless. We found and gave out ration cards to Jews so they could eat. Hundreds of people stayed in that little 'hiding place' at one time or another."

Eldorai waited for a guard to pass by before continuing. "And yet you are here. I assume there is a story for that."

Corrie nodded. "A man named Jan Vogel had shown interest in our work and asked if we could hide some Jews he knew. He acted sincere, but it was a trap, for he was a

---

6. The Gestapo were the Nazi secret police.

Nazi spy. He preyed upon my father's willingness to do anything for those the Nazis despised ... Jews, disabled people. Vogel used my father's sweet nature against him. Less than ten months ago, the Gestapo came to our house, arrested us, and we were sent to Scheveningen Prison. That's where my father died. Then Betsie and I were sent to Kamp Vught, then here. We are suffering for the sake of Christ, but He sees us. He knows us. And he loves us."

"And your Jewish friends?" Eldorai asked. "What became of them?"

"All safe. All escaped."

"How do you know?"

"Because of a letter I received soon after being imprisoned in Scheveningen. A little scrap of paper that said *'All the watches in your cabinet are safe.'* That is how I knew they survived and escaped. I was in prison, but God did a great work in saving them from the Nazis."

"Why do that," Eldorai asked, "if it placed you, Betsie, your father, your family in such peril? I understand a willingness to help others, but at such cost? You lost everything!"

Corrie swallowed hard. The memory of the betrayal and arrest was surprisingly strong. "Simply because," she paused as one of the guards made another circuit past their table, "the people we help are humans like anyone else. Our Jewish friends who stayed in our little 'hiding place'. The blind, the crippled, all those who were afflicted, they are children who are marked with the image of God. How could we turn our backs on them? And as for losing everything ... well. All I can say to that is you can never learn that Jesus Christ is all you need until He is all you have."

She put down the toggle switch and looked at Eldorai. "And if you and your Romani families had come to Haarlem, we would have given you the same shelter, the same help, the same love." She reached across the table and squeezed Eldorai's hand as her friend's eyes glistened with tears. "I want you to know that."

"Ten Boom!" One of the female guards barked as she approached their table. Corrie let out a sigh.

"I was merely encouraging my fellow prisoner," she calmly said, preparing for a verbal barrage from the guard. "Surely there is no crime in that."

"It has nothing to do with that," the guard hissed. Rapping the table with her baton, she waved toward the door with her other hand. "You are to go to the infirmary immediately upon request."

Corrie looked at Eldorai and nodded her goodbye. *Betsie,* she thought.

Less than a medical facility, the infirmary was a small, cramped building near the commandant's office, which was a short, slightly downhill walk from the workshop. Corrie stumbled into the dimly lit interior and took a moment to look around, eventually discovering her sister upon a bed in the far corner. Deep coughs and loud retches from the other patients split the air. It was no way for an infirmary to be run, thought Corrie.

For all her suffering, Betsie's face brightened upon seeing her younger sister approach the bed. Even the pernicious anemia that afflicted her all her life could not dampen her joy. Sputtering cough after cough, she managed to prop herself up on a pillow with Corrie's assistance, even taking a sip of water from a glass on the bed stand.

"I am so relieved they actually called you here," Betsie rasped, her vocal cords damaged from her incessant cough. "I wasn't sure if I would have the pleasure of your company."

"You doubt the authorities?" Corrie asked with a wink.

"You never know," Betsie smiled. She winced in pain and went off into another round of coughing, clutching her side as she finished. "I'm especially glad of seeing you today. It is not clear to everyone when the end draws near, but I can safely say now that God is calling me home."

It was hardly a surprise to Corrie, given her sister's condition, but hearing the words of finality escape Betsie's lips moved something deep within her soul. Bowing her head, Corrie began sobbing quietly as she held her sister's hand.

"Oh Betsie!" she blurted out, earning a scathing look from a nurse across the room. "Of course, I know that for you to pass into the Lord's presence is more wonderful for you. But how it saddens me nonetheless! I have never known a day of life when you weren't my sister ... "

"And I still shall remain your sister even when I am gone, dear Corrie," Betsie replied. "Death does not change that. It only delays reunion for a while. I'll be free of this shell of a body and receive a new body from my Savior, and I choose to see the future through those eyes! But I don't know how long the guards will allow you to stay, so please let me share what I have to say with you."

Corrie smiled through tears and bade Betsie to continue.

"I wanted to share with you that God has revealed things to me about what is going to happen. I have seen and received His message as clearly as I ever have before, and I want them to be my parting gift to you, sister. First, He has given me a vision of a house, and in this house there are prisoners who have been freed. Seeing to this will be your destiny, Corrie."

"But I don't know what that means!" Corrie insisted, gripping Betsie's hand.

"Nor do I exactly," Betsie continued, "but that will be for God to show you more clearly in time. Secondly, we cannot allow death and hatred to have the last word. God wants you to teach the Germans—even the ones who have shown such brutality to us and to our Jewish friends—

to love others as Jesus the Messiah loves us. May that endeavor be radical, dear Corrie. Once this wretched war is over, purchase a camp like this one and transform the grounds of hatred into a haven of love and grace."

"That is indeed a tall order, Betsie," said Corrie, "but I will try. And the third?"

"For what God has shown me, you will need to work quickly. Labor day and night leading our fellow prisoners in the Scriptures. Sing songs with them in the bunks. Pray with them fervently and lead as many of them to the Cross, placing their faith in Christ, as your strength allows. Because our release is coming before the end of year!"

"Our release!" mouthed Corrie, afraid of anyone overhearing the incredulous idea. "But you can't even rise from the bed! How can you be sure of your release, let alone mine?"

"I will be released to my Savior's presence before the New Year. My race is over, the fight is done. But God has shown me you will be released from here. Do not ask me how. It is enough to trust in Who will accomplish this. You will leave Ravensbrück alive. But you have little time to bring more sheep into the fold of the Good Shepherd, so be diligent!"

Corrie could not fathom the good news coming from her sister's mouth. The tears flowed again, and she pulled Betsie into an embrace. "I will do so, dear Betsie. In everything, I will trust my unknown future to my known God."

Betsie smiled back. "Yes, Corrie. Trust him always. For there is no pit so deep that Christ is not deeper still."

CORRIE TEN BOOM (1892-1983) lived out her faith in the midst of danger and death. Born into a watchmaking family in Haarlem, Netherlands, she assisted in the rescue and preservation of Jewish people under threat from the Nazis who occupied Holland during the Second World War. Arrested along with the rest of her family in February 1944, she lost her father and then her sister Betsie. Days after Betsie's death, Corrie was informed of her release from Ravensbrück concentration camp. Her release was actually due to a clerical paperwork error, and for this reason she was spared while many in her barracks perished in the gas chamber. After the Second World War, she ministered among war survivors and Germans, and in 1971, she wrote *The Hiding Place*, in which she told the story of the ten Boom family's rescue work.

FACT FILES

Christians in the Shadow of Evil

For Christians to endure in life, very often believers must trudge on from ordinary day to ordinary day. The mundane nature of existence can tire people out. However, at times, and in increasing fashion, Christians around the world find themselves living in very dire circumstances. Sometimes they are the victims of intense persecution and injustice. Other times, they must intervene and help others who are the targets of great evil or difficulties. One example of this is Baroness Caroline Cox (born 1937) who founded the Humanitarian Aid Relief Trust (HART) that brings aid to many who suffer oppression and persecution, including many Christians. But in the twentieth century, we find examples of many Christians who took their faith seriously. They not only believed you must place their faith in Christ, but that faith should also lead to action. At times, this meant making bold decisions when evil forces held power in their nation. Other times, some stood firm against the injustice and ugliness of racism. And others have been willing to face grave danger and even death because they loved Christ so much.

In Denmark, the Lutheran pastor and playwright *Kaj Munk* (1898-1944) spent twenty years as the vicar of the parish church in Vedersø[1]. Initially, Munk professed great admiration for Adolf Hitler, as he was greatly impressed by the Nazi's leadership and organization and wished Denmark could have a similar leader who could unify their land. However, as he became aware of the Nazi persecution of the Jews during the Second World War, Munk turned against Hitler. Not only did he speak out against the

---

1. Vedersø is a town on the west coast of Denmark near the North Sea. It is about a four-hour drive from the capital of Copenhagen.

evils of Nazism, but he also criticized from the pulpit his fellow Danes who would collaborate with the invading Germans. In spite of warnings from friends, Munk would not be quiet, speaking out on behalf of the Danish Jews and coordinating efforts to hide them in safety. In the end, Hitler was so enraged by the Danish resistance that he ordered their top leaders be targeted. The Nazi leaders in Denmark also banned evangelical preaching in the cathedral at Copenhagen. Munk ignored that order and preached an Advent sermon there in December 1943. One month later, as he was walking down a rural road near Silkeborg, Munk was shot to death by a Danish group of Nazi collaborators. He never was able to see the Allied victory, but his determination to demonstrate the Gospel that he preached emboldened many of his countrymen under the threat of evil, and he remained faithful even when he didn't see the results of his preaching.

Closer to the epicenter of Nazi cruelty, the German pastor **Martin Niemoller** (1892-1984) became known for his commitment to stand up against Nazism on German soil. After the First World War (in which Niemoller served as a submarine officer for Germany) and the collapse of the secular Weimar Republic, many Christians in Germany at first hoped the new chancellor Adolf Hitler would usher in a spiritual revival. But in July 1933, Hitler's administration levied two restrictions on all clergy: They had to be politically submissive to the Nazi government, and they had to affirm the superiority of the Aryan race[2]. Along with theologians like Dietrich Bonhoeffer (whose story we encountered earlier in this volume) and Karl Barth, a leading Swiss theologian, Niemoller saw through the Nazi order and spoke out against it. He declared the Church had freedom to serve God apart from political pressure and

---

2. The concept of the "Aryan race" was a false idea that designated the German people as a "master race" who were superior to others and viewed Jews, Blacks, Roma (gypsies), and others as subhuman species.

influence. While a number of the state churches accepted the Nazi demands, Niemoller was involved with other churches who opposed the regime. In January 1934, such like-minded leaders met in Barmen, Germany, to form the Confessing Church as the underground Protestant coalition that would oppose Hitler in faithfulness to Christ and not follow others who submitted to Nazism. Their stand was that true unity "can only come from the Word of God in faith through the Holy Spirit."[3] Niemoller's fervent faithfulness made him the target of the regime. He was convicted in a Nazi court for preaching a "rebellious sermon" and sentenced to seven months in prison. Hitler ordered him arrested almost immediately after his release for continued resistance, and Niemoller spent over seven more years imprisoned in concentration camps at Sachsenhausen and Dachau. In spite of his heroic stand, Niemoller often wished he could have done more and spoken out strongly earlier on behalf of those who could not defend themselves.[4] After the war, he became highly involved in the peace movement in Germany.

In the United States, while concentration camps and Nazi threats weren't an immediate factor, the nation was still grappling with the fact that racism, bigotry, and prejudice were ever-present factors in society. Basic civil rights for African-Americans were hard to come by even as many (such as Francis Grimke, discussed earlier) spoke out on behalf of Blacks. But one part of the American social fabric was professional sports, and in 1947, the

---

3. From the Barmen Declaration, the main document drafted at those proceedings.

4. In Niemoller's former cell in Sachsenhausen, there is a plaque with the words of his oft-uttered regret. In essence, it goes, "First, they came for the Communists, and I did not speak out, because I was not a Communist. Then they came for the social democrats, and I did not speak out, because I was not a social democrat. Then they came for the trade unionists, and I did not speak out, because I was not a trade unionist. And then they came for me, and there was no one left to protest."

Brooklyn Dodgers promoted **Jackie Robinson** (1919-1972) to their team, breaking major league baseball's "color line" and making Robinson the first Black major league baseball player in the modern age of the sport. While a talented player, Robinson showed tremendous strength of character as he endured racial epithets and abuse from fans and other players, not responding in anger but taking the moral high ground of decency and nonviolence. Part of this came from his Christian faith, even though Robinson was not often explicit about his trust in Christ. But since his younger days growing up in southern California, a muscular faith had taken root. Karl Downs, a minister at the Methodist church where little Jackie attended with his mother, challenged the youngster to place his faith in Jesus and for that faith to be an anchor in difficult times. During his time with the Dodgers, Robinson's speed, talent, and success demonstrated to onlookers the ability and equal human worth that he and all African-Americans possessed. Even as he dealt with racial abuse, he remembered Jesus' command in Matthew 5 to "turn the other cheek" and made that a regular practice. In the process, Robinson enjoyed a famed career, many awards, and an unforgettable world championship with his team[5]. Through his actions, Robinson began to transform the attitudes of a nation, preparing the ground for the civil rights movement that was to come.

Although we often think of martyrdom (being killed or executed because of one's Christian faith) to be a reality from ancient times through the Protestant Reformation, the truth is that more Christians have been martyred since 1900 than all the previous years of history combined. To

---

5. Robinson was the Rookie of the Year in the National League in 1947, the Most Valuable Player in 1949, played in six All-Star games, and was a member of the Brooklyn Dodgers' 1955 World Series champions. His number 42 was retired permanently (no other player can wear it as a jersey numeral) by Major League Baseball as a tribute to his legacy.

detail all of them would take many volumes, but we should mention some here. One bold disciple of Christ was **Chet Bitterman** (1952-1981), who knew that sharing his faith in hostile territory could be costly but answered the call to mission nonetheless. As a student at Columbia Bible College in South Carolina (now Columbia International University), Bitterman became highly interested in Bible translation work and connected with Wycliffe Bible Translators. After further training in linguistics, Bitterman married his wife, Brenda, and they were sent to the nation of Colombia in South America. Before they left the United States, Bitterman wrote in his diary, "I find the recurring thought that perhaps God will call me to be martyred for him in his service in Colombia. I am willing." Working at the Wycliffe base in Loma Linda and later in Bogota, he and Brenda eventually assisted other translators even as political instability and drug cartel violence swirled around their locations. They were preparing to move into the jungle to be with the Carionja tribe to learn their language in order to translate the Bible into their tongue.

On the morning of January 19, 1981, several M-19[6] Colombian soldiers invaded the facility in Bogota where the Bittermans were staying. Although the armed troops were looking for the director of the mission to use as a hostage, they kidnapped Bitterman instead. Holding him hostage for forty-eight days, the M-19's demanded that the Wycliffe translation team leave the country or Bitterman would be killed. Although negotiations for Bitterman's release went on, he did not want the team to leave when the Bible translation for the Carionjas wasn't complete. On March 7, he was shot to death by his captors. In answer to his prayers, as well as the prayers of his wife and friends, God's Word spread as a result of Bitterman's death. Bible verses from his letters during his imprisonment were

6. M-19 was another name for the 19th of April Movement involvement in a revolutionary struggle against the ruling political party in Colombia.

printed in Colombian newspapers. And applications to Wycliffe rose dramatically in the days following his death, as many young Christians volunteered to full-time missionary service, willing to go into dangerous habitats as Bitterman had.

Two years later, on the other side of the world, Christians experienced the outpouring of hate, terror, and death, producing a group known henceforth as the **Martyrs of Sudan** (May 1983). Sudan—an overwhelming-majority Muslim nation—was torn apart by civil war that took on an increasing religious flavor. The Christian minority in Sudan found themselves more and more under attack. The Muslim government in the capital of Khartoum was imposing full control over the nation, restricting freedom of speech and assembly, declaring Islam the official state religion, and stating that the criminal code would be based on Islamic Sharia law[7]. And they were demanding that Christians accept these realities.

On May 16, 1983, in the larger context of a two-decade-long civil war, a gathering of Christians—primarily from the Anglican and Catholic communities—declared they "would not abandon God as they knew him." Their resistance to the Islamic regime unleashed the full fury of Khartoum, and over the next two decades, well over one million Christians were slaughtered at the hands of Islamic militants. From that point until the civil war paused with a peace treaty in 2005, four million Christians were displaced from Sudan by the violence, scattering elsewhere in southern Sudan, in Africa and the world. In spite of the destruction of life, schools, and churches, relief came out

---

7. Islam is the religion of which Muslims are followers (see *Reign: The Church in the Middle Ages*; ISBN: 978-1-5271-0801-1, Christian Focus Publications, Ross-shire, UK: 2022). Sharia law is an interpretation of the criminal and civil code of a nation or people group that is based on the authorative sources of Islam in the Qur'an and the Hadith; some criticisms of Sharia law include the brutality of punishments and viewing women as less valuable than men, as well as restrictions on other religions like Judaism or Christianity.

of the shadow of evil. Those Christians who remained in southern Sudan benefited from the redrawing of political lines, as a new border was placed to create the new nation of South Sudan. Although for a time, there had been hardly any Christians in this area, now eighty-five percent of the people of South Sudan belong to a Christian church community. The trust of ordinary believers in God's mercy has sustained them through many days of sorrow.

Finally, some Christians are brought to the verge of martyrdom yet are saved from death and given freedom. The story of **Asia Noreen Bibi** (b. 1971) is one such example. In June 2009, Noreen, a Christian woman in highly Islamic Pakistan, was harvesting berries with many other women near the village of Sheikhupura. When asked to fetch water, she took a drink from a metal cup. The other Muslim women (Noreen and her husband were the only Christian family in the area) saw this and berated her, saying it was against the law for a Christian to drink from a vessel Muslims would also use. Noreen recounted that while the other women insulted her and demanded she convert to Islam, she calmly said, "I believe in ... Jesus Christ, who died on the cross for the sins of mankind. What did your Prophet Mohammed ever do to save mankind? [W]hy should it be me that converts instead of you?" In response, after she returned home, a mob came to her home and beat her and other members of her family. The next year, she was sentenced by a Punjab court to die by hanging for the crime of blaspheming Islam. Her husband Ashiq appealed the verdict, and the local governor—a Muslim— was willing to pardon her and have her released. But when the governor was assassinated and Noreen's imprisonment dragged on (in an 8' by 10' solitary confinement cell), all seemed lost. However, Christian and secular human rights organizations spoke out against her mistreatment and imprisonment, and demanded she be set free. The group Voice of the Martyrs collected 400,000 signatures from people in over a hundred countries, pleading for her release. Higher courts struck down the appeals, but her case kept going forward to the Pakistani Supreme Court. There, in October 2018, over nine years after her original arrest, the Supreme Court acquitted her of all charges of blasphemy. Later, she was able to leave Pakistan and settle in Canada with her husband.

For years, followers of Jesus face danger, abuse, and even the threat of death. But they must do so by following the call of their Savior, to face their trials faithfully.

BILLY GRAHAM

September 21, 1947, Grand Rapids, Michigan

The rain was unrelenting as the car hit a massive puddle on Lyon Street after the right turn off Monroe Avenue. Glad they had brought an umbrella, the evangelist wearily rubbed his eyes with both hands as their driver brought the car to a stop in front of the building. The rain wasn't the only thing that would not let up, thought Billy Graham as he gave his eyes one last massage. He had been preaching every day for the past week and his reserves were dangerously low. And now he was within ninety minutes of his closing sermon at this event with his body about ready to give out.

"The Lord has been working through you all this time," his friend and fellow evangelist, Charles, quipped from the seat beside him as he readied the umbrella for opening prior to what promised to be a mad dash to the doors. "I honestly am so grateful for how he has moved through your words over these days."

"As ever, I am humbled and grateful for your kind words, brother," replied Graham, tilting his neck from side to side in a vain attempt to loosen its tightness. "What I could use is for the Lord to work refreshment through my body for this last sermon so that my words will be effective."

Smiling, Charles fished inside his coat pocket and pulled out a bottle half the size of his hand. "Billy," he said as he opened the bottle, "I'm entirely sure that God works through vitamins to restore us in time of need." Shaking the bottle, he managed to drop a single pill into Graham's hand. "Vitamin C. Hopefully, it'll hold off any illness and give you a little pop of energy."

"One can only hope," Graham sighed. He looked through the windows and saw the rain wasn't letting up. "Well, no time like the present. Let's make a run for it."

Aside from jumping into a puddle that went up over their ankles just outside the car, both Charles and Graham managed to make their way up the stairs, rush between the middle two of the six pillars that fronted the Civic Auditorium, and then dash into the front lobby. Wiping his feet on the entry mat to dispose of as much water as possible, Graham looked around the interior. Ballroom staircases ascended up either side of the lobby, which was cast in an interesting ensemble of wood paneling and art deco design. When Graham first preached in the facility Thursday night, an usher mentioned how it had been built during the Great Depression, for the chief purpose of providing employment for local citizens. *May Jesus do an even greater work than that tonight,* Graham prayed. *But, oh Lord, I am so weary and I need your strength.*

They checked into the main arena, walked to the stage, and performed the battery of sound checks. The doors would open for guests in thirty minutes, and Charles was anxious to allow Graham to have time for sitting and relaxation before the auditorium would be packed. Admittance had been free to each of the crusade services since eight days before, and with tonight as the final event, Charles was sure the room would be overcrowded.

"Looks like the staff have provided sandwiches and drinks, at least," Charles quipped when he and Graham reached the hospitality room together.

Graham eased himself into a chair and stretched before reaching over and taking a sandwich. "More reason to be thankful," he said, chewing on a bite of roast beef and cheddar. "And even though we got our feet soaked getting out of the car, I'm sure you'd say amen to the fact that rain here in Grand Rapids is a big help."

"There's rain and then there's a super soaker like today," replied Charles. "I wouldn't be surprised if the golf course at the country club gets sodden enough that members complain they can't play tomorrow."

"Don't disparage the game of golf," Graham responded as he took a gulp of lemonade, the North Carolina accent evident in his voice. "I don't know if I told you this before, Charles, but golf has to do with how I was pulled to the pulpit."

"I don't think you told me that story."

"It was the golf club at Temple Terrace near Tampa," Graham said, a faraway look in his eyes. "I was at Bible college there and it was one of those afternoons. I was on the eighteenth green, finishing up a game of golf, and that's when I really sensed the Holy Spirit shaking me up. I had preached at churches before, but this was the time that God reached into my spirit and made it clear: He was calling me to preach his Word to as many as would hear it. That was what I was created for, and I prayed in that moment and believed him." Graham looked at Charles. "So there you go. Golf has plenty of uses."

Charles chuckled as they both heard a knock on the door. Cliff Barrows entered with several pages of sheet music in his hands. "Billy, I'm headed to the stage to warm up on the piano and give the people some gathering music," he said. "Any changes to the songs compared to the earlier plan?"

Graham got up and crossed the room. Together they spent the next five minutes going over the song selections, in low voices uttering phrases like, "That's a good choice" or "Perhaps we could shorten this for time, play three verses and not four". Finally, Graham said: "Just a thought,

Cliff. Let's try this." He thumbed through the selections until alighting on a page that arrested his attention. "This one. Let's invite them forward with this."

"That's excellent," Cliff answered, holding the sheet up as if acknowledging its surpassing worth. "We might have the new standard right here." Raising his hand for a brief wave, he added, "See you out there."

The two of them, Graham and Charles, were left alone in the room. Tenderly placing his hand on Graham's shoulder, Charles asked him, "Brother, how do you feel? In all seriousness, let me know. You've done so much in this event, this—what are we calling it?—crusade, that I praise God for your preaching and fervor. Do you have strength for one more service?"

"I will," Graham assured him. "No matter how weary I may become, my hope is this: It's not I who speak, but Christ through me. Let's pray these young people see Christ afresh this night, some for the first time."

Billy welcomed the crowd and began in prayer, and before he was through the word "amen", Cliff had already moved seamlessly into the first notes of their opening hymn. As if an unseen force moved them, the assembly rose together and joined in loud song:

> "O Lord my God, when I in awesome wonder
> Consider all the works Thy hands have made,
> I see the stars, I hear the rolling thunder,
> Thy pow'r thru-out the universe displayed!"

Graham stood by his chair, several yards behind the pulpit, singing the words but allowing their force to penetrate his heart. Slowly, he went from singing aloud to quietly mouthing the words and praying in his heart: *Yes, Lord,* he prayed. *You are the Great Creator. And tonight be the Wonderful Savior, and may many come to know your matchless grace.*

He opened his eyes. They had gone to the third verse, and Graham felt the love of Jesus well up within him.

> *"And when I think that God, His Son not sparing,*
> *Sent Him to die, I scarce can take it in –*
> *That on the cross, my burden gladly bearing,*
> *He bled and died to take away my sin!*
> *Then sings my soul, my Savior God, to Thee;*
> *How great Thou art, how great Thou art!*
> *Then sings my soul, my Savior God, to Thee;*
> *How great Thou art, how great Thou art!"*

Pressing his Bible between his hands, Graham prayed again, *May they know you, Lord Jesus. May they come to know and love you.* The voices rose on the final verse:

> *"When Christ shall come with shout of acclamation*
> *And take me home, what joy shall fill my heart!*
> *Then I shall bow in humble adoration*
> *And there proclaim, my God, how great Thou art!*
> *Then sings my soul, my Savior God, to Thee;*
> *How great Thou art, how great Thou art!*
> *Then sings my soul, my Savior God, to Thee;*
> *How great Thou art, how great Thou art!"*

It went that way for the next twenty minutes, singing and prayer. Graham not only saw the looks of spiritual need and hope on the faces of the people; he sensed God renewing his strength to preach one more time at the close of this crusade. Eventually, it was time for him to come forward and preach. As he bade the people to sit, he thanked them for the time they'd had over the prior week, encouraging them in their zeal to hear from God. Now, he declared, he wanted to remind them of one more glorious truth.

"I wish to take you to the Gospel of John this evening. Please open your Bibles together to John's Gospel and let's go to the first chapter." He thumbed through the pages of his King James Bible[1] until he found the text. "It is a simple moment we will enter into here, my friends, but it ushers in a deeply profound call to us. John, chapter one, verse twenty-nine. Here, John the Baptist stands at the Jordan River, baptizing people who were repenting of their sins against God, when all of a sudden, who should come to him … but Jesus himself? And we find these words: *"The next day John seeth Jesus coming unto him, and saith, Behold the Lamb of God, which taketh away the sin of the world."*

Graham placed his hands flat on the pages of his Bible, his eyes closed as if deep in thought when suddenly he opened them and raised two fingers. "This is not the end of a crusade, but the beginning of the remainder of your life in which you will live either for Jesus Christ or against him! This is a beginning. For some of you, tonight may be more of a beginning than you might reckon. But it begins by allowing this verse to confront us … and then to comfort us!"

Straightening himself, Graham looked around at the thousands in attendance. "Because God desires to do that to you, for you, through his Word tonight, there is something that you must be confronted about. Confronted, you say? I can hear you say, 'But this is a church service! This is a Youth for Christ[2] event! Why do we need to be confronted?' I'll explain. Better yet, I'll let John the Baptist explain!" He paused as his deference to John caused a ripple of laughter among the crowd. "John says that Christ, as the Lamb of God, takes away the sin of the world. That is not the problem of other people! That is our problem. That is your problem. Because a number of us in this auditorium tonight are living in the ways of the world. Sin moves us.

---

1. Graham tended to use the King James Version when he preached, although he was known to utilize other translations in his writing and personal devotions.
2. At this time, Graham was an employee of Youth for Christ International. It was formally organized by Torrey Johnson (who hired Graham) in 1944, with its goal being evangelism among young people throughout the world.

Rebellion against God drives us. We love ourselves, but ignore Christ. And we need that posture corrected. If that is you, you need your mind changed. You need your heart transformed, washed of the filth of sin. You need what keeps you from God taken away."

Graham allowed the words to sink in. Charles watched from behind and Cliff Barrows listened from the piano as Graham went on. "But how? You can't do it. Oh, you might say, 'I can keep the rules. I'm a moral person. Isn't that enough?' Let me explain: Keeping God's moral code is good, but you cannot keep it in the way you should. The apostle Paul even describes what that is like. It's as if you are looking into a mirror. You can see that you've got a dirty face But you cannot use the mirror to clean your face; that'd be ridiculous!" He pointed to several in the front row. "You, when you have a fever, do you check the temperature with a thermometer? Yes? Good. But the thermometer will only tell you something's wrong. The thermometer can't heal you."

Walking back and forth behind the pulpit, Graham grew more animated. *Quicken their hearts, Lord,* he prayed silently. He went on. "And that is the beauty of this text. Through John, he shows us our need, one that we cannot rescue ourselves from. But when we have no hope in ourselves, we see God provides a way! God has provided liberty from our rebellion, cleansing from our filth, he accepts us in spite of our disdaining him, and he does this through a Lamb! You see, in the days before Jesus, in ancient Israel, God's people would have to bring a lamb from their flocks. And these lambs would be slaughtered and placed on an altar and offered to God, so God might forgive the people's sins. The lamb was necessary, for that sacrifice demonstrated what the people could not do themselves."

"So when John identifies Jesus as the Lamb of God, he was not only speaking to the people gathered at the river with him! God was speaking through him **to us** today in this room!" Graham's words had the effect of a thunderbolt, and some people in the auditorium leaned forward in their seats and began weeping. "I ask," he continued, "are you weary of your effort of never being good enough? Are you despondent that you have something deep within— your sin—that keeps you from a relationship with Jesus Christ, who is the only one who can change your life and make you beloved by God? If you say, 'Yes, I want that relationship with Christ', I have good news, the greatest news, which John shares here! Jesus himself is your provision! His death was the sacrifice that washes the filth of our sins away and cleanses us. And he is the same Jesus who stretches forth his wounded hands to you, and he bids you to place your trust in him, to put your faith in him, to come and receive him into your life, so your life may be changed by him!"

Cliff Barrows leaned into the keys of the piano, notes lilting through the expansive room and people wiped tears away and bowed their heads, many singing softly.

> *"Just as I am - without one plea,*
> *But that Thy blood was shed for me,*
> *And that Thou bidst me come to Thee,*
> *O Lamb of God, I come! I come!"*[3]

Graham gestured toward the front area of seats and said softly, "If you wish to give your life to Jesus, your Savior, your Lord, just come forward. Your past may be a ruin, but in Christ your future is one of hope. Come as you are, weeping, hopeful, however you come. But if you need Christ, just come."

And they came.

---

3. This is the first verse of Charlotte Elliott's hymn "Just As I Am", which became a frequent song at Graham's future crusades when people would come forward to make public profession of their faith in Jesus Christ.

The Baptist evangelist **BILLY GRAHAM** (1918-2018) preached the first of his many crusades [which he called "missions" after 2001] in Grand Rapids, Michigan, that day, launching a ministry that would take him around the world. Arguably one of the most influential Christian leaders of his time, Graham preached in over one hundred and eighty countries on six continents. An estimated 3.2 million people prayed for salvation through Christ at these meetings. Articulate and wise, Graham also had an audience with twelve different U.S. Presidents. His passion for worldwide evangelism, racial reconciliation, and Christian discipleship gave him a platform in many countries and enabled him to offer the Gospel clearly and directly. Above all, his greatest love was for Jesus Christ who had saved him and called him to service.

C.S. LEWIS

February 1948, Oxford, England

"Jack[1], I really don't know why you're determined to have dinner there," complained Owen Barfield, "when the Lamb and Flag across the street has much better food, not to mention a delicious steak and kidney pudding!"

His companion waved off the rebuke as they passed the Martyrs' Memorial in St. Giles' Street and marched on through the wintry mix falling from the heavens. "Rubbish!" C.S. Lewis said dismissively as his steps gained more vigor at the thought of a good meal. "The trouble with you, Owen, is that you are willing to change a gathering place with no thought to tradition. Not to mention that prying Tollers, Warnie, and Hugh loose from the Eagle and Child is more than you have strength for."

"You and your poetic disdain for anything else," replied Barfield, shaking his head vigorously to dislodge the evening's moisture as they approached the Eagle and Child public house. "Although I have to say sitting in the room with good friends in decent warmth grants one a more joyful view of the world."

"Moving words for an Englishman," Lewis replied as they drew near the door of the pub. "Any more emotion and you shall have us all swimming in a river of our own tears." He opened the door and gestured his friend to

---

1. C.S. Lewis went by the nickname 'Jack'. When he was four years old, his beloved dog Jacksie died and Lewis began using the late dog's name, unwilling to be called anything else. Eventually, Lewis accepted the name Jack, which family members and friends called him throughout his life." (from Irene Howat, *Ten Boys Who Used Their Talents*, Christian Focus Publications, 2006).

enter. "Besides, I think we might have somewhat of a surprise tonight."

"You're late, Jack," announced J.R.R. Tolkien—the "Tollers" of the group—as Lewis and Barfield entered the well-lit room and shuffled to their seats. "Certainly a professor who likes his students to arrive early can persuade himself to get to dinner on time."

"I am neither early nor late, Tollers," Lewis chuckled, waving away the smoke curling from Tolkien's pipe, "because I arrive when I wish to arrive." He sat next to his friend. "What's with the look on your face?"

"Nothing," Tolkien responded, "other than you are quick-witted as always. Have you ordered yet, or do we need to do that for you, as well?"

"I saw Hugo going to get drinks," Owen Barfield said, referring to their friend Hugo Dyson, "so we asked him to put in requests for our pies."

"Excellent choice for a cold and rainy evening," piped up Warren Lewis, C.S.'s brother—whom the group called Warnie—setting his glass down on the table, careful as always to put it exactly in the middle of a napkin laid flat.

"Still can't let go of your military discipline, Warnie?" Lewis remarked.

"You can take me out of the army, but you can't take the army out of me!" exclaimed Warren, with the slightest of nods.

In time their food arrived at the table, and for the next forty minutes it was the usual conversation about their latest readings, notable questions and insights from students at Oxford, and Warren gushing about their garden at home.

"You're quite cheerful whenever you speak of the gardens at the Kilns," noted Hugo. "And although I'd rather lecture than write, your words almost move me to drop by for a visit and inscribe some poetry about your blessed flora."

"I always keep telling you to write more," Tolkien quipped, bringing a chortle from Lewis.

"That's because you are *always* writing more," Hugh responded, "and at least we were spared any more of your wandering fantasy ... "

"Because you kept complaining," said Tolkien.

"Because your stories are so conking long!" Hugo blurted out. "That one you were sharing from, what was it? *The Lord of the Rings*? Surely publishers might be put off by its sheer length."

"What you might not realize," Tolkien sniffed. "is that those with whom I've shared it, happen to like what they read."

"All right, gentlemen," said Barfield, ever the peacemaker, holding up both palms as a calming gesture. "Let me remind you we don't gather to throw dirt on the past but to talk about what we are doing now. So, what has anyone been writing recently, and do you have any copies to share around the table?"

Lewis took a gulp of his drink and promptly stood. "I don't have copies of my latest endeavor, as I first want to be further along in my labors. However, I have just had an idea, or rather the re-invigoration of an old idea, take hold within my imagination. And when your imagination is baptized with wonder, you take that new life wherever it might lead you."

"You and your sacramental language, Jack!" Hugo smiled.

"Most appropriate, I'd say," Tolkien said. "The only cure for the sagging of fainting faith is Holy Communion. Why wouldn't we expect a revival of imagination along similar lines?"

"You would say that, Tollers," Hugo teased, earning a hard look from Tolkien.

"Can we get back to what Jack has to share about his book?" Barfield said, noticing a young man at the door of the room eavesdropping with a curious look.

"Thank you, Owen," Lewis sighed before staring into the middle distance, a strange look in his eyes. "The story is more of a children's tale, markedly different from what I have written before. It was the one I began at the time of the war. You remember, about the children who had to leave before the Blitz?"[2]

"Yes, Jack, you shared that with us," said Tolkien, cleaning his fingertips with a napkin, "and as I recall, we criticized it a great deal and you gave it up. I know I probably said more than the others, but you didn't need to set it aside for such a long time."

"True," said Hugo. "You did give him more critique than all of us combined."

"But that doesn't need to stop Jack," Tolkien continued, waving his hand encouragingly toward Lewis. "I am sure this new draft bears the marks of great improvement. Am I correct, Jack?"

"The eye of the beholder will judge," Lewis continued. "When I first envisioned this story, I saw in my mind's eye a faun. Yes, a faun, and he was walking, strolling ... well, skipping, really. He went through a wooded place carrying parcels. There were children in that story, initially called Ann, Martin, Rose, and Peter. I remember that like it was yesterday. However, the lot of you were so relentless in your criticism that I shredded it, yet," and here Lewis winked at Warren, "the story never truly left me. And recently I had the most incredible vision of a new character leaping right into the story, bounding in both uninvited and yet as if he owned the tale, for he is what binds the entire story together!"

"Who is this man?" asked Barfield.

"Not a man, a lion!" Lewis replied with delight. "His name is Aslan, and he is the ruler of the entire world."

---

2. The Blitz that Lewis refers to is the Battle of Britain, when the Nazi air force (the Luftwaffe) relentlessly bombed Great Britain, and especially the London area, from July through October 1940. A number of children were sent away from London for their own safety prior to that time.

"A world in which the entire story takes place?" queried Hugo.

"No, the children—whom I've renamed Peter, Susan, Edmund, and Lucy—travel there."

"How?" Tolkien asked, a pained look on his face.

"The only way you can," Lewis responded, clapping his hands together. "By magic!"

Immediately, the group nodded in agreement and surely would have been the challenge for Lewis the rest of evening, if not for something else. For at that precise moment, the young man from the doorway—the one Barfield noticed earlier—let loose with a loud guffaw, his laughter doubling him over and his momentum carrying him into the room. Barely holding on to his drink glass, he pulled himself together and smiled broadly at Lewis, tipping his hat in his direction.

"By magic?" he said. "Heavens! I heard rumors that you were quite the showman, but I never imagine showmen would speak through their hats in such a manner!"

"And that's as far as you go, whippersnapper!" ordered Tolkien, rising from his chair and pointing back to the main room. "You're intruding on our area. Inklings only!"

"Now, now, Tollers, I don't think he's wise to our group's traditions," interrupted Lewis. "I am not certain how much a showman I could be, and talking through my hat might be a matter of perspective, but that's just me." He offered his hand. "C.S. Lewis, with a hail and well met to you."

The stranger, taken aback by Lewis' affable nature, returned the handshake. "Patrick Steel. Pleased to make your acquaintance."

"And you've met Tollers here," Lewis replied, gesturing at Tolkien. "And at the table with us are Hugo Dyson, Owen Barfield, and my brother Warnie."

"No need to introduce Professor Dyson," said Patrick with a kind wave to Hugo. "He's my tutor for Shakespeare."

"Is that so?" Barfield exclaimed.

"Patrick here is a regular contributor in my lectures at Merton," said Hugo. "Here on a Rhodes scholarship, is that right? From New York?"

"Graduated from Hartwick College and matriculated here," Patrick said, raising his glass. "I just never believed I'd be in the company of such intellect."

"Then, might I ask why you decried my understanding of getting somewhere else by magic?" Lewis inquired.

"Me?" Patrick spluttered, taking a seat which was offered by Tolkien. "In a scientific age, it's so odd to hear someone of robust academic temper to speak freely of getting somewhere by hocus pocus."

"Is science going to be that effective?" asked Lewis.

"Here we go," Warren said, reaching for his glass and licking his lips in anticipation of the impending clash of wills.

"I was just going to say," continued Patrick, "that science has been effective at showing us what is true."

"True as in accurate or true as in right living?" Lewis pressed him.

"True as in right living?" Patrick scoffed. "Don't tell me you're going to bring all that morality stuff into this?"

"Is that wrong?" Lewis replied, his brow furrowing in mock concern.

Tolkien tapped Hugo on the leg and grinned, whispering, "I know you and I can disagree at times, but this is one thing we really enjoy!" Hugo nodded his assent.

"Of course, it's wrong to do so!" Patrick blurted.

"Wrong?" Lewis responded. "As in morally wrong?"

"I'm simply saying that the old ideas of right and wrong, fairness and injustice, are just things we piece together," Patrick insisted. "We make them up as we go, as we say across the pond."

Lewis paused, the slightest of smiles playing at his lips. He turned to Barfield and asked, "Owen, what chance is there the bar can spare us a cup of coffee?"

"Wonder what he has planned with this?" muttered Barfield to Warren as he stood up to go to the bar.

Lewis tapped his fingers on the table and looked at Patrick's rucksack, pointing at one of its contents. "Bit of a football fan, are you?"

"What?" asked Patrick, following the direction of Lewis' finger. "Oh, that. Yeah, that's a match program from last weekend. Got away for a—uh, football match, what we in the States call soccer. I played at Hartwick, so I wanted to view one here."

"Barbaric term, soccer," grumbled Hugo as Tolkien raised his eyebrows.

"Where was the game?" Lewis asked.

"Oh, one of my mates is a Swindon Town fan," Patrick began, "so we caught the train up to Burslem[3] and watched them play at Port Vale this past Saturday."

"Good game?"

"Energetic. Port Vale won on a single goal. Worse game than some, but better than most."

"And did they run around outside the pitch, pick up the ball, throw it into the stands, kick it around Swindon?" asked Lewis.

Patrick's face registered complete surprise. "Why would they do that?"

"Couldn't they?"

"No," Patrick retorted, "it's against the rules. The game wouldn't make sense! A match like that wouldn't be right, it wouldn't be football, it ... "

"Beware, Patrick," Lewis said gently. "It appears you are making an argument that we need rules, as if there is a law of decent nature that keeps things in line. I'd say this is universal in the heart of everyone." Lewis nodded his thanks to Barfield as he returned to the table with the coffee. Rising from his

---

3. Burslem is a town near Stoke-on-Trent in the West Midlands of England. Approximately a three-hour train ride from Oxford, it is the home of Port Vale Football Club.

chair, Lewis grabbed the cup and took a step toward Patrick, ready to tilt the cup and pour the coffee over his head!

"Now what are you doing?" shouted Patrick, causing patrons at the nearby tables to crane their heads in his direction.

"I was just going to pour this over your head," Lewis said, a smile tugging at the corners of his mouth. "Not allowable?"

"You can't do that!" Patrick huffed.

"Because it would stain your clothes?" Lewis sighed.

"Because it would burn me! No one does what you were going to do!"

"It sounds to me like you are saying it's not right, it's not fair, it would be harmful, it would be wrong," said Lewis, "so maybe the idea of decency, of right and wrong, good and bad, is more universal than you allowed."

"That hardly seems the point of it all," Patrick growled, humiliated by his own vulnerability. "Why don't you just prattle on about morality and be done with that?"

Lewis replied, "Whose morality? That of the Jews? The Hindus? Jesus? Islam?"

Patrick eyed Lewis warily. "I'll go for the direct approach and let's debate Jesus' teachings."

"Who do you mean by Jesus?" Lewis said, sitting back down and crossing his hands behind his head. "Are we both talking about Jesus Christ, the eternal Son of God, God who became man, Savior of sinners?"

"You know better than to expect a rational man to agree to that," Patrick insisted. "You really want to go back sixteen hundred years and have a collection of dead men dictate who Jesus was?"

"Is."

"Professor Lewis, I refuse to believe that you want to throw your lot in with a bunch of Bible-thumping fundamentalists on the Jesus question."

"I think they would not be seen with me in a place like this," Lewis quipped, "but let me ask you who you think Jesus is?"

"Why are you interested?"

"Jesus was interested in Peter's response. I'm interested in yours."

"We all are," Barfield said quietly, and Tolkien raised his glass in his direction.

"Just what can we confidently say about Jesus?" Patrick said, tugging nervously at his jacket as he sat. "He was a good man. A great moral teacher. One can even say he had an exquisite command of truth and morality. But as to what you claim about him being the Son of God? About being God? No. He was good. He was moral. That was it. I'm just being honest."

"Begging your pardon," Lewis said slowly, "but I don't think you are. I'd say you are being profoundly *dishonest* about who Jesus claimed to be."

"Dishonest?" Patrick spluttered.

"Yes, Patrick. Think about what Jesus did when he was on earth. He said he had always existed, and he said that to Jewish people who believed God was the only eternal being. He accepted worship and honor given only to God. And he forgave sins, other people's sins!"

"So what? I do that all the time when others wrong me!"

"But think how staggering that is! When Jesus forgave the sins of a paralytic, he forgave his sins against all sorts of people. If I insult Tollers over there, and Warnie here forgives me for that, is that reasonable?"

"No," Patrick allowed, "because your offense is against Professor Tolkien, no one else."

"And yet that's precisely what Jesus does," Lewis replied excitedly, "in acting as if he is the one ultimately offended by all sins. He is claiming to be God himself, wouldn't you say?"

"Why are you pressing for a decision?" Patrick frowned, sitting bolt upright in his chair.

"Because I am trying to prevent you from saying the one thing you shouldn't say about Jesus, that you accept him as a moral teacher but reject his claim to be God," Lewis replied, leaning into the space between them. "Patrick, think about it. A man who was only a man and said the things Jesus did would not be moral, let alone a good teacher. Maybe he would be crazy like a man who came running through this pub claiming to be a fried potato. Or he would know he was merely a man and claim to be God and thus be the most horrific liar in the history of humanity. So yes, that is why I am pressing you for a decision, because that is the honest thing you must do. Either Jesus is the Son of God, or you should say he needed to be in an asylum, or you should admit he is the most deceptive soul in history. But stop the patronizing platitudes about him being a great moral teacher. Jesus himself does not give you that option. So you must decide."

A blanket of quietness rested over the group, until Patrick set his own glass on the table, stood to his feet, and rasped, "I need to go." As he put his derby hat on, he muttered, "I have some thinking to do."

As Patrick walked out of the room, Hugo looked at Lewis. "Well, Jack," he said, "do you think he'll convert?"

"He now has a stone in his shoe, and he will feel that if he wishes to walk onward as before," Lewis said before smiling broadly. "But if God has him in the meshes of a net of hope, I doubt Patrick is going to escape."

The British writer and literature professor **CLIVE STAPLES LEWIS** (1898-1963) struggled through the difficulties of losing his mother at a young age and beholding the horrors of the Great War. But the once-skeptic embraced belief in Christ and rose to fame as a thinker who communicated clear, robust reasons for the Christian faith. His wartime addresses for British Broadcasting Company radio formed the basis for his book *Mere Christianity*, in which he made a reasonable case for historic Christian teaching. Many of his other books sought to make a case for biblical truth or morality, such as *Miracles, The Problem of Pain, The Abolition of Man,* and *The Screwtape Letters.* His Space Trilogy of *Out of the Silent Planet, Perelandra,* and *That Hideous Strength* cemented his status as an outstanding science fiction writer. Lewis is also much loved for his children's novels in *The Chronicles of Narnia* series, and his marriage to Joy Gresham is the focus of the 1993 film *Shadowlands.* Above all, Lewis is widely revered for his ability to take deep Christian ideas and make them understandable for inquiring minds and hearts.

FACT FILES

Popular[1] Apologists of our Day

Virtually all of us have done something we've had to face up to, a matter for which we've had to say "I'm sorry." Perhaps you ate a slice of pie in the refrigerator that was reserved for someone else in the family, and you had to confess your greed. Maybe it was something more serious, like chasing your brother or sister through the house so fast that they fall and get injured, and then you have to apologize to them and your parents for doing so (hopefully not in the emergency room at a hospital!). For us, that is the essence of the expression, "I apologize." We are admitting regret for doing something wrong, something reckless, maybe something sinful, and we are owning up to our responsibility.

While all of the above is true, when it comes to being an *apologist* in the Christian sense, we move away from the sense of saying, "I'm sorry" into a different realm. The task of what is called *apologetics* is to take seriously the questions and challenges toward the Christian faith and give credible, reasonable answers as to why Christianity makes sense out of everyday life and presents the truth about reality. While apologetics has developed rapidly in recent years, it has a very long history. Justin Martyr debated with others in the second century A.D. and even had a lengthy correspondence with a Jewish thinker named Trypho, defending Christianity from the accusations of

1. In this title, the word popular does not mean 'commonly liked' or 'widely loved and approved'. It means 'able to be understood by a larger group of people'. Popular apologists are able to take complex ideas and questions about the Christian faith and then explain them in clearer and simpler ways to ordinary people. There are also Christians who are apologists in a more academic environment who are more understood by scholars (Cornelius Van Til, etc.), but the goal of this chapter is to give readers a sampling of thinkers whose primary concern is a larger audience of ordinary people.

others.[2] During medieval times, churchmen like Anselm of Canterbury sought to show why Jesus as completely divine and completely human made perfect sense, and Thomas Aquinas gave compelling arguments for the existence of God.

Recently, however, as the world becomes more strongly secular[3], a number of followers of Jesus have committed themselves to serious apologetics. They desire to confront the questions and skepticism of people who take issue with the Christian faith, tackling those matters head-on, and then crafting answers to those questions while asking questions of the secular mindset. You have just read about C.S. Lewis, who was gifted in this regard, and later you will encounter Francis Schaffer and his work at L'Abri. Yet there are more apologists who have arisen who have delivered quality work in this area.

One individual who has been on the front lines of the relationship between the Christian faith and questions of science is **John Lennox** (b. 1943). Born in Northern Ireland, Lennox carved out a distinguished academic career as a mathematician who specialized in group theory.[4] In 1962, while a scholar at Emmanuel College, Cambridge, he happened to attend the final lectures of C.S. Lewis, who was speaking about John Donne's poetry.[5] The young Lennox was impressed by Lewis' command of faith and Christian doctrine and was convinced that

---

2. See my *Redemption: The Church in Ancient Times* (Christian Focus Publications, Ross-shire, UK: 2022), 75.

3. "Secular" here would mean a belief that God is either non-existent or irrelevant. In short, it can be a code word for "non-religious".

4. In case you are interested, group theory is a field of modern algebra that, as my friend Robert Murphy says, studies the patterns and shapes which are part of real and imaginary objects. For example, a Rubik's Cube is a pattern-machine where we might see the interrelatedness of ways to get from one presentation of the cube to another. Group theory is the language used by mathematicians to describe those transformations and connections (from email response from Robert Murphy to the author).

5. Donne was an English poet and writer in the sixteenth and seventeenth century known for such works as "Death Be Not Proud" and "No Man Is An Island", among other works.

the Christian faith made sense out of academic study. As Lennox continued on in his work, gaining master's and doctoral degrees in both mathematics and bioethics, he saw the world as a dynamic, glorious tapestry created by a loving and sovereign God, and this brought meaning to everyday life. He taught mathematics at the University of Wales, Cardiff for a number of years, as well as lecturing at Oxford on the relationship between science and the Christian faith. It was his work in the latter sphere that brought him into dialogue with other Christians and open debate with skeptics. Lennox has participated in debate with atheists such as Peter Singer, Richard Dawkins, and the late Christopher Hitchens on topics of ethics, the existence of God, and the positive impact of Christianity. In doing so, Lennox demonstrated a civil and kind tone in his approach, valuing the questions of his critics even as he debates vigorously with them. Lennox has written books defending the Christian faith, such as *Christianity: Opium or Truth, God and Stephen Hawking: Whose Design is it, Anyway?,* and *Can Science Explain Everything?*

While Lennox gives coherent reasons for Christianity as a scientist, other apologists have come from other backgrounds than academics. *Lee Strobel* (b. 1952) served as an award-winning newspaper journalist for the *Chicago Tribune* and *Chicago Daily Herald* for nearly a decade and a half. Strobel was known for his tenacious investigative work. He was also a convinced atheist, and when his wife Leslie mentioned she had embraced the Christian faith, he decided to investigate the claims of Christianity as a journalist would. Certain that he would expose Christianity as a fraud, he was surprised to discover the events of the Bible held up to scrutiny, and Strobel became a believer himself. He has since served as a teaching pastor at churches in Illinois, California, and Texas, as well as hosting a show *Faith Under Fire* while remaining much in demand as a speaker. Strobel is most known for his apologetics books that interview thinkers across North America regarding Christianity, demonstrating that biblical faith is solid and credible. Among these books are *The Case for Christ, The Case for Faith, The Case for a Creator,* and *The Case for Easter.*

Yet another apologist who came from skepticism to faith is **J. Warner Wallace** (b. 1961). Wallace was a confirmed atheist who served as a police detective in the Los Angeles area, assigned primarily to cold cases.[6] When Wallace was thirty-five years old, he began to explore the New Testament Gospels, applying cold-case investigation techniques to see if the Gospels could stand up to such pressure. In time, Wallace came to believe that one could trust the Gospels were reliable historical documents and that Jesus Christ truly and literally rose from the dead. Wallace launched an apologetics ministry to teach people why Christian belief is reasonable and meaningful. He has broadened beyond his initial investigation of the New Testament to the Bible as a whole, engaging with a wide variety of topics while appearing on many television and news broadcasts. His books include *Cold Case Christianity* (his original investigation into the reliability of the Gospels), *God's Crime Scene* (evidence for God creating the universe), *Alive* (evidence for Jesus' resurrection), *Person of Interest,* and *Forensic Faith.*

While the above personalities came from backgrounds in the university, journalism, and criminal justice, *Tim Keller* (1950-2023) demonstrated how a pastor might lead the way in apologetics during the process of ministry. Keller became a Christian while a student at Bucknell University through InterVarsity Fellowship. After gaining

---

6. Cold cases are criminal investigations—mostly homicides or kidnappings—that have not been actively pursued for some time because the case lacks evidence. A cold case detective then might take up the case to see if compelling evidence exists or may lead a team to investigate a cold case if new details emerge.

his seminary degrees, Keller pastored a church near Richmond, Virginia for nearly a decade before moving with wife Kathy to New York City to launch what became Redeemer Presbyterian Church. In the process of ministering to young urban skeptics, Keller would preach and teach with a healthy dose of apologetics. His sermons and presentations would anticipate questions that unbelievers would have, respectfully demonstrate where the pressure points and problems were in a skeptic's way of thinking, and then offer the Christian way of life as a true, noble, reasonable, and beautiful alternative. An author of many books on Christian thought and living, Keller has also penned two works particularly apologetic in nature: *The Reason for God* and *Making Sense of God: An Invitation to the Skeptical.*

And thankfully, we are seeing the field of apologetics is not exclusive to male leadership. In recent years, a number of women have risen to places of leadership and innovation in the apologetic field, seeking to provide ways for ordinary Christians to think through the implications of faith compassionately and clearly. **Mary Jo Sharp** heads up the ministry known as Confident Christianity. Sharp encourages Christians to share and defend their faith through very reachable strategies. First, know what you believe and why you believe it. Then, listen to people, and be able to articulate, dignify, and understand their doubts and questions about Christianity. Be prepared to ask questions, not just quote Scripture at people who would likely reject the Bible anyway at first. Ask them, "What do you mean by that?" or "How do you know that to be true?" Then you are in a position to respond, and to build a good relationship through these extended conversations with others. **Nancy Pearcey**, who learned much through the ministry of Francis Schaeffer at L'Abri in Switzerland (see the chapter on Francis and Edith Schaeffer later on), is a writer and professor at Houston Christian University. Her book *Total Truth* offers correction to what she calls the fact-value split. Pearcey notes that many people believe religious faith is based on values and feelings, while science and reason are lodged in fact. In truth, she says, the Christian faith has credible support and is shown true by good thinking skills. Like Sharp, Pearcey believes in listening well to the questions and objections of doubters, who have value because they are created by God, and that should drive our compassion toward them. "You have to love people enough," Pearcey says, "to listen to their questions and do the hard work of finding answers for them."

In all, apologetics is an enterprise of great contributions from committed Christians, as those involved in it know the value of deep roots of what one believes joined with a wide reach that seeks relationships and helping people make sense out of life. That should direct our thanks to God, who continues to raise up people equipped to engage the world and help change it for Jesus Christ.

ELISABETH ELLIOT

January 1956-October 1958, Ecuador

The rain abated, but the clouds remained overhead. *Perhaps that will bring some cooler weather with the cloud cover,* thought Elisabeth as she looked out at the trees of Shandia. Somewhere beyond them, her husband and his four friends[1] were likely praising God for the gift of a foothold for the Gospel. Elisabeth smiled as she thought of all the planning that had gone into this endeavor. For a few years, their group had been laboring among the Quechua tribe, finding progress slow but steady as more of the natives were responding to the sweetness of Christ's message. God had blessed their actions and they were seeing a dedicated band of disciples sprout among the men, women, and children of the Quechua. But Elisabeth knew that even as God caused things to grow where they were planted, her husband Jim believed God could call them to more.

"The Huaorani need to see the love of Christ, as well, Betty," Jim urged her one evening six months ago, using her preferred name as he cradled little Valerie in his arms. "Yes, they are hostile, but there are so many divisions among their tribes that foment that hatred. I really believe that the cross of Jesus will heal the divisions and their warring can cease."

"You never stop believing," Elisabeth smiled, "do you, Jim?"

---

1. The "husband and four friends" were the following, with their wives' names in parentheses: Jim Elliot (Elisabeth), Nate Saint (Marj), Peter Fleming (Olive), Ed McCully (Marilou), and Roger Youderian (Barbara).

"Not for a second," he said before kissing her softly and looking down at their daughter. "Isn't she precious?"

Her precious daughter whimpered and cried, bringing her back from her memories.

Elisabeth put down her cup of coffee and rubbed her eyes. She had not been able to sleep much the night before. Marj hadn't relayed news of the men's contact with the Huaorani. But since she couldn't dwell on that, Elisabeth began the morning routine of getting Valerie out of bed.

"The Lord is good," she whispered, quoting the prophet Nahum, "a stronghold in the day of trouble."

Elisabeth Elliot had no idea how real those words were about to become.

She had finished feeding Valerie about seven-thirty when the radio crackled to life. Handing Valerie off to Nate's sister Rachel, who was staying at the Elliot home for a few days, she snared the receiver and offered a loud "Hello?"

"Betty?" It was Marj.

"Go ahead," Elisabeth replied. "What do you know? What did Nate say about the meeting?"

"That's just it," came Marj's response, one that betrayed tears. "We never heard from him at four-thirty when he promised contact.

The trickle of worry from the lack of news burst into a flood of fear at those words. "He never contacted you?" Elisabeth asked.

"No," Marj said. "Olive is with me and she can verify that. And Marilou and Barbara are in Arajuno, of course, and they have received no word on their end."

"Perhaps the radio wires weren't well connected," Elisabeth offered, desperate to explain why no report had come. "Have you tried that?"

"We did within fifteen minutes of when Nate was supposed to radio in," came the breathless reply of Marj Saint, betraying irritation mingled with increasing worry. "The connection was fine, and it's set to the frequency Nate mentioned, so whatever is wrong with the transmission, it's not on our end. Olive checked the plugs again and everything was in working order. The same thing went for Marilou and Barbara."

Elisabeth prayed silently as she waited while Rachel, wide-eyed, bounced Valerie on her knee. Finally Marj said, "Betty, are you still there?"

"I'm here."

"We waited past seven yesterday evening. I mean, Nate is sometimes late with making contact, but this is beyond even that. I thought about contacting you, but I wanted you to at least have a chance for some sleep."

"It might not mean they're in danger, or that anything has happened to them," Rachel said, cradling the whimpering Valerie in her arms.

"That's true," agreed Elisabeth. "Their radio might not be functioning. It's been known to happen before."

"I know, Betty," Marj sighed. "but I'm just worried because if something has happened, there's nothing to fall back on for help in the moment. Nate was so excited to have made the contact with the Huaorani and this meeting seemed to be coming together, but they were going in alone and didn't want any help. Didn't even take weapons for defense, nor have they told many in our network they were going in."

"So did you not tell anyone?" Elisabeth panted. Feeling dizzy, she sat down as Rachel brought Valerie over and sat next to her. The room seemed to be spinning.

"Art Johnson came in last night and saw me with my head down on the desk by the radio," Marj replied, her voice cracking. "He asked me what was wrong and I told him. I didn't want him to go public with it. If nothing has happened to the men, crying danger would not be the thing we want to announce. But he and I talked to Johnny, and he left about a half-hour ago to fly in and find them. He knows where to go. On an earlier flight, Nate pointed out the sand strip where he planned to land yesterday."

"I hope Johnny stays safe, as well," Elisabeth said. She had confidence in Johnny Keenan, who like Nate was a pilot in the MAF[2]. She took a deep breath and, feeling more stable, continued. "Now, Marj, my offer from last night still stands. What do you need me to do? I have to teach my literacy class to some of the village children right now, but I can be available by nine o'clock."

"Perfect," Marj said. "Johnny might be reporting back by then. Can you stand by in case there's word?"

Woodenly, Elisabeth agreed, then switched off the receiver. "Rachel, I still need to teach my class. Can you take Valerie for me?"

Rachel nodded wordlessly, tears spilling down her cheeks. Elisabeth ascended the stairs to the classroom loft where the children would be waiting. Waiting, that was, for their teacher who would take great pains to conceal her breaking heart.

"When thou passest through the waters, I will be with thee, and through the rivers, they shall not overflow thee," she whispered Isaiah's words.

She opened the door to the excited greetings of the students, and her heart silently offered another prayer. *Lord, let not the waters overflow.*

But overflow they would. It was nine-thirty when Marj's voice crackled on the radio with the news they all dreaded. "Johnny has found the plane on the beach. All the fabric is stripped off. There is no sign of the fellows."

---

2. The MAF is the Mission Aviation Fellowship, an organization founded after the Second World War which provides air travel and communications to many Christian missionaries and other humanitarian groups. Nate Saint was an early member of the group.

For months afterward, the world's attention shifted to Ecuador and the reaction of five widows whose missionary husbands had been speared to death by Huaorani warriors. As the widows processed their grief together, the questions lingered: How did it happen? Was it an ambush? Did they proclaim Christ to the warriors, who in that moment felt threatened by the confidence the men had in Jesus? What of our children, who face the coming days without their fathers? These were questions that had no immediate answers. One could only trudge on, and Elisabeth had to do that as well. She was doubly determined to stay on in Shandia to minister to the Quechua, regardless of where the other wives would go, wherever the Holy Spirit would scatter them for the future. But what shape would her ministry continue to take?

She could never have imagined how God would make that answer crystal clear to her. It was on a visit to Marilou's house in Arajuno in November of 1957, while Valerie was taking her afternoon nap.

"Betty," came a voice from the dining room door. Marilou entered the room and padded to the table, seating herself across from her friend. "What are all these letters and cards?"

"It's helpful to me to see how Jim, Nate, Ed, and the others were remembered," Elisabeth answered, reminding herself that the other women felt grief at an abject level as she did. "It reminds me of how the body of Christ is truly worldwide. People who never knew Jim or Nate or Ed or Roger or Peter, and yet they've inspired so many who have encouraged us so much." She picked up a card and showed Marilou. "Look at this, signed by an entire group of children at a church in Alaska. 'We love you and pray God will hold you close.' And this one, from students at a college in Japan. 'We are praying for you.' Even when things seem darkest, these letters bring light to my heart."

Marilou smiled and touched Elisabeth's hand. "One of my favorites was that letter addressed to me, from that missionary on the Nile River. She had opened up the issue of *Time*[3] and saw Ed's picture and broke down crying. She was a friend of his from America, and she couldn't believe he was gone. Her letter was filled with so much hope and Scripture. And she hoped we would press on in the work here."

"That is what the Quechua are praying toward," Elisabeth marveled, "and not merely that we stay among them, but that we be willing to follow our expressions of forgiveness and seek out others in their tribes, or even the Huaorani ourselves and proclaim Christ to them, for maybe they will listen. You know that Rachel has been working with Dayuma, the Huaorani woman who escaped from their village? Dayuma has become a believer in Christ and Rachel has been learning their language. We are hoping perhaps it leads to an opportunity to return to them."

"It would be an amazing chance, to minister to the ones who killed our husbands" Marilou replied.

"I have sat among the Quechua over the past weeks," said Elisabeth, "as they cry for us as well, even nearly two years on, but they constantly ask what can be done for the Gospel. One of them, who used to be enslaved to alcohol, said to me 'Senora, I lie awake at night thinking of my people. How may I reach them? How will they hear of Jesus? I cannot get to them all, but they must know! I pray to God, asking him to show me what to do!' And so many of them prayed just last week to bless the Huaorani. They prayed, 'Lord, send more messengers to go to them. Give them soft hearts instead of fierce hearts. They pierced our friends, but Lord, you can pierce them with your Word, so they might both listen and believe.'"

---

3. *Time* is a magazine. The American media devoted significant coverage to the tragic deaths of the missionaries. Also, *Life* (another pictorial magazine) did a massive photo essay detailing the missionary work and the tragedy.

Elisabeth looked up to see Marilou smiling, wide-eyed. "What is it?"

Marilou stood. "This is why I came to you just now. I want you to experience some answered prayer. Come with me."

The wait to return to Shandia tried Elisabeth's patience as her heart was bursting with exuberance, and when she saw Rachel and Dayuma sitting at the dining room table when she walked in, she threw down her cases, ran to them, and scooped both women up in an embrace.

"Hello to you, too!" Rachel exclaimed. "But why the fierce hug?"

"Because of something that Marilou shared with me when I was in Arajuno with her!" Elisabeth exclaimed. "And I couldn't wait for you and Dayuma to get back so that I could return and give you the news!"

"What news?" asked Dayuma in her broken English.

Elisabeth could barely contain herself, covering her mouth with her hands and then pulling them away as she gushed, "When I was at Marilou's house, she told me two Quechua women in the village came to speak with her. They were housing two Huaorani women who had escaped from their tribe." She looked at Dayuma. "Their names are Mankamu and Mintaka. I don't know if you knew of them, but they had heard of you."

Dayuma began crying, her hands shaking. "Praise be to Jesus!" she wept. "I haven't seen them in twelve years. What did they say?"

Elisabeth took a deep breath. "Rachel, Dayuma ... let's ask them ourselves." She nodded toward the front door and two women entered cautiously into the dining room.

Mintaka raced into Dayuma's arms, the two women crying loudly until Mankamu joined the embrace. In the midst of it all, Elisabeth and Rachel could hear words exchanged. Even with Rachel having learned some of the

Huaorani language from Dayuma, it was difficult to make out the exact exchange. "Dayuma," she asked, "what did they say?"

Dayuma smiled through tears and said, "They said, 'What you have, they desire to have, and they know it is the only hope of their people.'"

Almost another year had gone by, months of intense learning, training, and prayer. Through it, Dayuma had grown in her faith and Mankamu and Mintaka had been cleansed by the blood of Christ, as well. And they were not the only ones to mine the treasures of these days. Rachel and Elisabeth learned the Huaorani language in enough depth that they had made the decision to go dwell among the Huaorani tribe, one that in those dark days of January 1956 they would not have believed possible.

"We're absolutely sure of this?" Rachel asked, knowing what Elisabeth's answer would be. Their boatman had taken them down the Curaray River and pulled ashore. Disembarking, Elisabeth stepped in the sand and looked into the jungle, praying for the days ahead.

"We have prayed that Dayuma, Mankamu, and Mintaka have been blessed in their return and have paved our road for us," Elisabeth said quietly. "Yes, I am certain. As surreal as it is, I know this is God's calling for us. We are finishing the work Jim, Nate, and the others began. That is what God wanted."

"Your faith always inspires me, Betty," Rachel replied, lifting a backpack and handing another to her friend.

"God is the one who inspires us to serve him," Elisabeth corrected her, cinching her backpack over her shoulders and taking Valerie by the hand. "This is no accident. God performs all things according to the counsel of his will. What is at stake is greater than the tragedy of two years ago. He always desired to bring us to this entrance into hope, to bring to these people the Gospel of Jesus. For he is worthy. He not only died for us, but for the Huaorani. And now we get to be part of his desire, that we bring his redeeming love to people of every tribe and tongue and people and nation."

She looked amongst the trees and she saw a man, a Huaorani, approaching them. And he was smiling.

She smiled back. "And it begins with us today."

Missionary wife, teacher, and writer, **ELISABETH ELLIOT** (1926-2015) demonstrated forgiveness and unconditional love as she ministered to the very people who had killed her husband Jim and four other missionaries in January 1956. She remained with the Huaorani (also called the Auca Indians) for two years, a time which brought spiritual growth and transformation to the tribe. She wrote of the events in Ecuador in the classic book *Through Gates of Splendor*. Eventually returning to the United States in 1963, Elisabeth became a highly respected speaker and writer. She also participated in the radio program "Gateway to Joy" from 1988 to 2001, and continued to offer wisdom and encouragement to new generations in the Christian faith. Elisabeth Elliot died in 2015 and entered the presence of the Savior whom she so greatly treasured and loved.

FRANCIS AND EDITH SCHAEFFER

February 1956, Huemoz-sur-Ollon, Switzerland

Her dirty blond hair disheveled, Molly shot her right arm forward, then her left, pulling her massive backpack upward behind her. The gravel path was thankfully dry and so she had no worries about solid footing, but the incoming snowy weather could change that. She had heard several people outside of the café in Huemoz discussing the weather. When in an unfamiliar place, she reasoned, trust the locals about the weather. She groaned as her back ached while she negotiated the incline, but as she looked upward she saw the chalet. That brightened her spirits considerably. Finding extra energy to push onward, she covered the remaining distance in less than five minutes and entered the property.

Even for a midwinter afternoon, Molly expected there to be more signs of life than the couple of people who milled about within her line of sight. One, a young girl who appeared to be well shy of Molly's twenty years of age, was placing a bulging bag in a refuse bin on the side of the chalet. Shaking her hands and then gently blowing on them to warm up her digits, she looked up and saw Molly approaching. If the sight of an ex-university student laden with an oversized backpack and clad in a sweater and dungarees surprised her, she didn't show it. Shortening the distance between them, the girl raised her hand.

"Greetings!" she said, smiling broadly. "I'm Susan! Have you come to stay here at L'Abri?"

Initially taken aback by Susan's exuberance, Molly hesitated, then warmed to the kindness in her voice. Nodding slightly, she said, "I am. That is, if you'll have me. In a way, I both am and am not sure what I am doing here. But perhaps I can sort that out. That doesn't sound strange, does it? My name's Molly, by the way."

Susan giggled, then extended her hand to Molly. "Not strange at all. You might be surprised how many people said that—or close to it—over the past few months." She shook Molly's hand, then waved her toward the chalet. "Come on in and we can get you settled and you can meet my parents."

"Your parents?" Molly asked, admiring the girl's self-confidence.

"Yes, Mother and Father oversee things," Susan replied, casting a glance at Molly's backpack and focusing on a patch. "That's an interesting item," she said, pointing to it. "That crest with the P-A-R-F-C beneath it. Is that a hand holding an anchor coming out of a crown?"

Molly's eyes lit up. "You're quite bright, Susan," she said. "Yes, it is. The P-A-R-F-C is Plymouth Albion Rugby Football Club. My father follows them and they tend to be my favorite team. It's their official crest." They walked into the main room of the chalet and Molly saw several logs ablaze in the fireplace. "Ah, what a difference it makes to come inside."

Susan smiled. "Come, I'll see where my parents are."

Molly did not imagine she would encounter the director of L'Abri in a back room with piles of wood, tools, and shavings strewn over the floor. The gentleman, whom Susan introduced as "my father, Francis", smiled welcomingly and bade Molly to sit with him while Susan went in pursuit of her mother.

"I trust Susan was a helpful presence upon your arrival," Francis said. He was a short man with kind yet penetrating eyes. He wore breeches and a long shirt in the drafty room, and his jawline was smooth and rounded. Gripping a long piece of wood, he quipped, "My latest project. I find it helpful to make a new walking stick every so often to get around."

"That is a wonderful skill to have," Molly replied. "My father's hobby actually."

"Is he a woodworker?" Francis asked.

"Of sorts," said Molly. "I'm from England, from the southern coast, in Salcombe. It's a beautiful tourist destination, has a yachting and sailing port, and my father works there as a shipmaster. But he is always making items in his shop to accent the ships' interiors, and he is quite a craftsman. I tended to spend time with him and made some knick-knacks of my own before heading off to university."

"Would you like to try your hand at something now?" Francis asked, nodding toward the corner. "There are some nice large aspen branches over there from which you could start fashioning a walking stick of your own, if you'd like."

"Are you sure?" Molly asked, surprised at her own comfort in being around this man as much as she was by his kindness.

"That is what they are there for," Francis said, sanding his own staff and blowing the dust onto the covered floor. "Find one that is as high as your armpit as that will be at the size you need. I have a small knife here with which you can whittle away at the bark."

Molly went to the corner, sized up the sticks, and returned with one that seemed the right size. "How much whittling should I do?" she asked.

"Enough so that you can see the wood grain, then no further," Francis said. "Once the whittling is done, which will take a bit of time, we can set it aside to dry. So," he continued, changing the subject, "you are from Salcombe but you say you went off to university."

"In Exeter, yes," Molly responded. "I am three terms into my biology course, but sometime in late October, I became very disillusioned. I had little desire to continue the course. Not that it wasn't valuable, but I had so many questions."

"About your course of study?"

"About life, really. I could read biology and do what was required, but I became aware I was confronting more than that. I had serious questions. Big questions. Why are we here? Who are we? What does it mean to live a good life and how do we know when we are on the right track? We asked questions at university all the time but they were about phylla and species, how to dissect in the lab, how to collect data from soil near the coast. To me, especially lately, they haven't been questions that matter."

"Which means your latest questions have been particularly effective," Francis said quietly.

"I don't understand," Molly said, puzzled.

Francis brushed the fine sawdust from his project. "You're here at L'Abri, aren't you?"

Molly grinned. "And I am speaking with someone who looks incredibly comfortable making a durable walking staff. That wasn't what I imagined when I came up the path."

"Oh, that happens to be the result from my upbringing," Francis assured her. "I grew up outside of Philadelphia back in the States and my father was an electrician. That meant a childhood of helping him with any sort of manual labor. I could fix pipes, change wires, saw wood, build things. My father would have placed a healthy wager of money on my following in his footsteps."

"So what happened?" Molly asked. "I mean, it's clear you work well with your hands, but here you are at a place that confronts questions and abstract details."

"It's true my parents wanted me in a more practical trade," Francis said, "but one day I was at an electrical show and I passed a display from another tradesman. I heard, floating through the air, the sounds of a song from a broadcast system. It was Tchaikovsky's '1812 Overture' and it absolutely gripped my spirit and embraced my heart. From that point on, I couldn't get enough of classical music."

"Then, also when I was in my teenage years, a member of our church—we were not a religious family, but we attended to keep up appearances—asked me if I could tutor someone. There was a Russian count who had emigrated to our area, an escapee of the Russian Revolution, and so I agreed to tutor him in English. I ordered a textbook for that from a nearby bookstore. But when I received the book from the owner, he had—by mistake, it seems—sent me a book on Greek philosophy. It might have been his error, but it was exactly what God designed!"

"How so?" asked Molly, whittling away at the bark, which was coming off the shaft in thin strips.

"It forced me to confront these 'big questions' you speak of, Molly," Francis answered. "And as I read more, I had a crisis of belief, followed by an awakening. I didn't think I could believe Christianity at all, yet I wanted to discover something. The Greek philosophers like Socrates, Plato, Aristotle, and Ovid ... they were all asking grand questions, needful questions! But they provided no satisfying answers. So I picked up a Bible and began reading it interchangeably with the Greeks for about half a year. And the most amazing thing happened: I realized philosophy was asking the right questions, but the Bible provided the story of the grand answers that could satisfy my heart. It told me about what this world was like, how we got to the places we are, why we do good, and why we are so morally fractured, as well. It made sense of what I encountered around me, and it gave me solid meaning for life. I was thirsty with questions; the Bible provided the water I needed!"

Susan appeared at the door. "Mother is in the sitting room and said you both could join her for tea there, if you wish."

"That sounds wonderful," said Molly, looking at her staff and glad of her progress, while her own mind was spinning with what Francis had just shared.

Francis' wife, Edith, poured the milk in Molly's cup, followed by the steaming tea and passed the cup to her. Molly had briefed her on her background that she had already shared with Francis.

"We're so happy to have you here, Molly," Edith grinned, leaning back on the sofa with their eldest daughter Priscilla while Francis settled himself in an armchair next to her. "And you are so gracious to excuse our mess around the chalet. We actually began L'Abri a few months ago and so there's a lot around here that will seem unsettled for a bit."

"What was it that inspired you to begin L'Abri?" asked Molly. "And why do you call it L'Abri?"

"It's French," said Francis with a wink as he adjusted the cuff of his trousers, "meaning 'the shelter'. It's what we hope it becomes for many people who come here with authentic questions."

"We came here as missionaries from America," Edith continued, "and it wasn't as if we left there with no regrets. Francis had been a pastor at a church in St. Louis, and we began a wonderful children's ministry there. We saw so much good come out of it. We had young people over for picnics, had summer Bible camp weeks, and also managed to have spiritual retreats that were structured yet fun. And that's when we noticed that young people have the most penetrating questions. They are searching for hope and significance beyond themselves. Sometimes they have difficulty putting what they mean into exact form, but we also discovered that the more we gave them a place to vocalize their thoughts, conversation would follow."

"That must have been an enormous undertaking!" Molly exclaimed.

"That was at a time," Francis added, "when we discovered that what is needed is not a lot of money to fund things, or organizational skill. We prayed a lot and just offered ourselves to God in whatever way He chose to use us. And then all these children in our neighborhoods became a part of that willingness."

"So why did you leave the States to come here?" asked Molly.

"Actually, I'd say God had planted something in my heart about a decade ago," Francis replied. "I toured Europe soon after the war ended. I saw the devastation of what the Nazis had done in Germany, but also the wreckage of property and souls throughout Europe. I would go to museums during the day and see the pain and suffering that lingered elsewhere. I believed that people in these regions needed the hope which the Bible offered their hardship and anguish. So we came here eight years ago as missionaries, to speak to others about the Christian faith. And that is when God showed He was still listening to our prayers. We didn't know what He wished to do, but we prayed constantly for God to show us."

"How did He do that?" asked the intrigued Molly.

"Well," Priscilla smiled, speaking for the first time with a confidence that made her seem more mature than her eighteen years, "you could happily blame me for that." She leaned forward. "Not even—what was it, Mother?— two years ago, I was in school here in Huemoz and several of my friends were going through some rough waters, you might say. Some were thinking about what the future held, and they asked some serious questions so I thought, 'These would be the exact people Mother and Father would enjoy!' I asked them to come over, and in the course of several weeks and many meals together, Father talked them through a lot of their problems. He showed how the Bible makes sense of life. They were asking questions and Mother and Father helped them follow the clues the Bible gave them."

"That is what gave birth to L'Abri," Francis said, "and the approach we take is the same: Pray, offer ourselves to God, and trust He will bring us people who wish to seek the truth and ask the questions on their hearts."

"Are you saying I am an answer to prayer?" Molly replied.

"One of many, I'd say," answered Edith. "We have others already who live here. We eat together, talk together, and work together. You'll help prepare meals, make things, beautify the property, or whatever you are gifted at doing. There are no little labors."

"Just as there are no little people," Francis added. "Everyone here, indeed everywhere, has tremendous dignity and value. We want you to be welcome. You may not feel it now, but we hope you will feel an increasing sense of family here the longer you stay."

"And you really don't mind my questions?" Molly inquired to make certain. "The fact that I don't know what I believe? That I may believe nothing at all?"

Francis leaned forward and smiled again. "We *adore* questions here, Molly. We are not scared by them. We know what it is like to have questions, to have confusion tugging at our hearts. And we want you to feel welcome. And perhaps in time, you will come to see that Jesus welcomes you, too."

FRANCIS and **EDITH SCHAEFFER** began the ministry of L'Abri in Switzerland in 1955, making their alpine home a haven for spiritual seekers from all over the world. Their compassionate relationships with others, combined with a knack for conversations built around the deep questions of life, resulted in transformed lives for many of their visitors. Using these principles, the Schaeffers were able to show that the historic Christian faith could be reasonably defended. Their generous and kind atmosphere at L'Abri influenced many, and Francis extended L'Abri's reach through many of his writings, which included *The God Who is There*, *No Little People*, *True Spirituality*, *Whatever Happened to the Human Race?*, and *He is There and He is Not Silent*. After a long battle with cancer, Francis died in 1984, with Edith following him into eternal life in 2013.

ETA LINNEMANN

January 1986, Batu, Indonesia

The students filed into the chapel, their murmurs of conversation kept low as they entered the sanctuary area. Looking north, they could see their classroom building, a reminder of the diligence it required to train as proclaimers of Christ's Gospel. The view of the building, though, was distorted by the pouring rain. That was no surprise given that January was the wettest month in Batu. The chapel itself featured a carpet up the middle aisle, which led to a raised platform and a pulpit. Only the pulpit had been removed, much to the confusion and consternation of several students.

"What have they done with the pulpit?" one asked.

Another frowned. "What does it mean? I thought we were here for the preaching of the Gospel?"

A third student, obviously serving in a leadership capacity, walked up to the two inquirers. "Rest easy, my friends," he said. "This is a special chapel and it will be lengthier than the ones we usually have. We are having a professor testimony and in order to grant some relief from having to stand too long, we are placing a chair where the pulpit was."

"That makes it all very well and good," said the first student, whose name was Jendri, "but who is it?"

"You seriously don't know?" came the reply.

"This is my first year," said Jendri, "so I am still getting to know the faculty. Sorry for being ignorant."

"That's no sin," grinned the other student. "I think you are in for a treat." He walked to the front of the chapel and raised his hands before calling out to the assembly. "Good morning, brothers and sisters in Christ! The Lord be with you!"

"And also with you!" called back the congregation.

"Permit me to pray," said the student leader, "and after that I will introduce our speaker." The entire student body bowed their heads as one as he began. "Lord Jesus Christ, we pray that we would honor you today as we behold your work through the lives of your servants. You have graciously drawn us from the kingdom of darkness and brought us into the kingdom of your glorious light. May we be encouraged today by the passion of your Gospel within the hearts of those who love you. In your holy name we pray, Amen."

Jendri was expecting a well-tailored male professor to ascend the platform. He was surprised to behold a woman make her way across the stage to the chair. Clad in a navy blouse and gray skirt, with a cream-colored scarf around her neck, she looked out at the applauding assembly through rounded eyeglasses. Upon seating herself, she adjusted her spectacles before sweeping her hand over her right temple and smoothing a strand of her graying hair, which was neatly parted near the center. Taking a microphone from the side table next to her, she smiled and began.

"Good morning, students, in the name of Jesus Christ who shed his blood for us," she said in a noticeable pronounced accent. "My name is Eta Linnemann, and our esteemed principal has asked me to speak in today's chapel service." She nodded to the side, where the principal nodded back. "In doing so, we had considered that I open a passage of Scripture and explain and apply it to you. However, upon further thought and given recent events, we thought perhaps it would be best to do so in this manner, a straight chat among friends in Christ."

She slowed down at the end of the last sentence, as if to emphasize the final three words.

Shifting in her chair, Eta continued. "I wish to share this time with you students and faculty today because of something that will be public. Well, that's not entirely true. Those who know me well already know my story. However, this will be even more open in the months to come as my journey of faith will be published as a book. I do not anticipate that my words will be received warmly by everyone, especially by my former academic friends back in West Germany[1]. But—and you will learn this as you minister in Christ's name in this land—truth must win out over acceptance. I have written a book that details my realization of my teaching. For years, I believed I was truly teaching what the Bible said. Less than a decade ago, the Holy Spirit brought me to the understanding that I was not."

Pausing briefly, Eta continued. "In a way, I feel at times like the apostle Paul did in the third chapter of Philippians, filled with everything that truly falls short, that truly doesn't matter, and I had to renounce it all for the surpassing glory of knowing Christ. Let me be clear about that. *Of ... knowing ... Christ.* I was teaching about the Scriptures, but I did not believe in the Jesus of the Scriptures, because of what—at that time—I believed the Scriptures were!"

"I want to give you my testimony today," she went on, "because I do not wish you to fall into the trap in which I found myself. I worked with people whom I revered. I do not know if you know the names of Rudolf Bultmann and Ernst Fuchs. No?" She smiled at the uncertain looks on many of the first-year students. "Their names are revered

---

1. Although Germany is a unified nation now, from May 23, 1949 to October 3, 1990, it was divided into West Germany (the Federal Republic of Germany) and the Communist state of East Germany. Linnemann is referring to the environment at the university in Marburg, West Germany where she had taught.

back in my homeland. Several years previously, I labored with them, looking at the Scriptures and in particular, the Passion narratives." She held up a hand. "Now. You are studying the Word of God here yourselves. Quiz time!" She called out, eliciting a laugh from the student body. "What do we mean by the Passion narratives?"

A student, three rows in front of Jendri and across the aisle, raised his hand and stood. "The records in the New Testament Gospels about the final week leading to Jesus' death."

"*Zehr güt,* as we would say back home," Eta chuckled. "Indeed you are correct. Now, you all would say the study of the death of Christ is a good one, yes?" She waited for the requisite nods and affirmations. "Not the way we approached it!" She paused for the gasps from the students. "From the very beginning, Drs. Bultmann and Fuchs ... and myself, I would add ... were determined to show that the Passion accounts in the Gospels were not only different, but they were also incoherent. They were contradictory. And we could have no confidence that these accounts gave us the truth about Christ or could stand as God's revelation to us. For the three of us, it was impossible to see that God was speaking truly in the Word because we had discounted His reality. The idea that we were sinners in need of a salvation through Jesus by His death ... that was discounted from the start. Why? Because we believed we were not separated from God, but that our world was separated from the improvement that could come if we followed the general principles of the Bible, which we viewed as man's words about God, not God's Word to us."

Taking a sip of water from a glass on the side table, Eta scanned the audience. "To be fully honest, I can go on and on. Are there any questions that might help shape this into more of a conversation?"

The principal raised his hand from the south wall and asked for a microphone. "Professor Linnemann, you might not wish to answer this, and you have full right of refusal to do so, but I'll ask: At that point, you believed those things about the Bible. Now you see that teaching was false. How did that affect the way you lived your life? Were there any devastating consequences?"

"An excellent question, sir," Eta replied, smiling. "And an important one that I need to answer, because all of you," and here she pointed to the students, "need to remember that our beliefs have consequences in our everyday existence. If we follow truth, then we will have lives that—no matter the difficulty—will be marked by God's grace and wholeness. If we follow what is false and twisted, then we will inevitably fall into patterns of living that are harmful and devastating. The more I kept defending the indefensible, the worse my life became. This is something I admit with no small amount of shame. I turned to alcohol with such dependence that my recovery was particularly difficult. I would sit in my flat evening after evening and drink to forget my increasingly meaningless study and watch television. To my acquaintances and friends, I appeared to be living my dream of scholarship, but what they couldn't see was that I was crumbling inside myself."

The student leader who had spoken to Jendri before the service stood respectfully and raised his hand. "Professor Linnemann, what to you was the essence of the flawed nature of your study?"

Eta looked very grave for a moment, stared into the middle distance, then straightened up in the chair and said, "Very simply, it did not take seriously what the Bible says about itself. I was taught that the words of the Bible and the thoughts of God are not identical. And thus the Bible is treated like any other book. The Qur'an of Islam. The Bhagavad Gita of Hinduism. The *Odyssey* of Homer.

The dramas of Shakespeare. The Bible is no more special than those works, I was told, and so I believed for some time. I am convinced that became the essence of my crisis. I couldn't trust anything the Bible said. I'll demonstrate why that is. Someone, anyone … select a verse from Scripture. Anyone. Say it out loud so we all can hear!"

A woman from the front of the assembly stood and piped up, "John 3:16!"

"An excellent choice," Eta complimented her. "and the passage I would have selected myself. John's Gospel, the third chapter, the sixteenth verse. *For God so loved the world that he gave his only begotten Son, that whosoever believes in him shall not perish, but have everlasting life.* Would you all agree that is what this verse says?"

The students all nodded in full agreement, while Jendri smiled with anticipation. *She is going somewhere with this,* he said to himself.

"Well, the tradition in which I was mired would say this: That is nothing more than mere human opinion. It would be what we hope for. But it is not a promise from God. It is not a binding covenant statement about our abiding hope. It is an opinion of a first-century writer who may or may not have spent time with a man named Jesus. That was the critical approach, the waters of which I drank deeply, the lake where God himself had to rescue me from drowning. Do you see where this leads? I ask, where does this lead?"

Jendri surprised himself by rising to his feet to answer the question. "It means one cannot trust that God has spoken. It means we cannot trust his promises. And if we cannot trust there is a God who makes and keeps promises, then we cannot truly trust anyone for certain!"

Eta looked at him from the front and smiled broadly. "You have judged correctly, young man. And what would you say to those that say it doesn't matter? That the Bible contradicts itself? What if someone told you the Bible contradicts itself, like in the case of the Passion story?"

"Quite plainly," Jendri responded, "I wouldn't say those stories contradict. There are different details, but wouldn't we expect four writers like Matthew, Mark, Luke, and John to tell the truth in a variety of ways?"

Eta brightened up and leaned forward. "Your words excite me. What do you mean?"

"If there is a robbery at night in a nearby shop," Jendri went on, "the local police might ask questions of different bystanders. One might say he heard the breaking of glass of the shop window. Another might offer that she looked at her watch when someone ran from the store in the darkness and saw it was ten minutes until midnight. A third may say he noticed a large man running south down the street. And another could swear she was in the shop, heard loud shouts, and then saw a man take something and run. Those are four different stories, all telling what they saw, and we would have no reason to believe they are lying. The truth is there was an event, and they were true witnesses. The Gospel writers say different things, but none contradict. They draw us into the life and death of the Lord Jesus, and that is where we must follow."

Jendri was not prepared for what followed. A round of applause burst in the chapel, and the principal took the stage. "Perhaps," he said, "we can take a break of ten minutes and continue this talk?" No sooner were the words out of his mouth than Professor Eta Linnemann had descended from the stage and come to Jendri's side.

"Bless you, Jendri," she said, shaking his hand vigorously, "for the Holy Spirit has revealed this to you."

"Bless you, Professor Linnemann," Jendri replied, "for coming here to Indonesia to teach us."

"Teach! Well ... " she said, eyes shining, "I could have used insight like you shared years ago. But thanks be to God, he changed my heart nonetheless."

In an academic culture of criticism and skepticism, **ETA LINNEMANN** (1926-2009) experienced the work of Christ in her life as she studied the Bible. In the mid-seventies, she repudiated the stance of her teachers Rudolf Bultmann and Ernst Fuchs after a conversion moment in which she embraced Jesus as her Savior. Urging readers to throw all her former books away, she went about her teaching career with renewed vigor, defending the reliability and authority of the Bible, helping to train new generations of Christian leaders to faithfully read and interpret the Bible. She continued to teach in Indonesia for a number of years while maintaining a residence in her native Germany.

J.I. PACKER

October 2002, Vancouver, British Columbia, Canada

"Remarkable," the driver uttered to no one in particular. "An open parking spot ... who would have believed it?" Carefully maneuvering his green Saturn SL-2 into a space on the eastern edge of the lot, he pulled the parking brake and turned off his vehicle. Looking up at the stone-and-glass structure before him, he reached into the passenger seat and grasped the packet of information before stepping out of the car and making his way toward the building. As he did, he let out a sigh of wonder.

"Regent College. Amazing," he muttered to himself, "this school is all under one roof. I feel crazy just coming here. So why do I sense something greater than myself is drawing me in?" Shaking his head, he told himself to stop making his inner dialogues so audible. Anyone he met would wonder about him, he chided.

Walking around the building and on to the main floor, he nearly dropped his parcel as a kind-looking bearded figure walked out of a bookstore head down, only avoiding a collision at the last second.

"My pardon!" said the man in a calm, reassuring voice. "I'm terribly sorry to have almost run into you." Looking more closely, he asked, "Can I help you? Are you a student here? I only ask because I've met almost everyone and you don't look familiar."

The young man nodded. "I'm a prospective student and I was coming for a campus visit." Extending his hand in greeting, he continued, "I'm Jordan Herron. I was asked to meet with President Wilson upon my arrival."

His newly met acquaintance laughed knowingly. "Good timing, Jordan! I'm President Wilson. Call me Rod, please. You caught me on my way back to the office. Just follow me and we'll be there before you know it."

"Didn't have trouble finding us in the sprawl of the UBC[1] campus?" asked Dr. Wilson once they got seated in his office.

"Just drove over from Burnaby. I'm in my last year at Fraser[2]. I play football there, and we were just over here last week to play UBC."

"Yes, you won that game, too. Ah, Jordan ... I remember your details now. So you are graduating in the spring?" Dr. Wilson asked Jordan. "And you are interested in pursuing further study here at Regent?"

"I am, sir," Jordan replied, finding it hard to use Wilson's first name even though requested. "I know I'm to sit in on an afternoon class, but I was hoping to meet some of the faculty before then and ask questions about the school."

"Indeed," Wilson responded, looking at a file on his desk that was marked with Jordan's name. "And I hope you will find a lot of your questions answered. We'll arrange for an official tour, of course, and facilitate you meeting others and soaking up the experience. But there's another matter, a bit of a surprise, actually. There is someone who wants to meet *you*."

"Me?" Jordan said, surprised. "But I don't know a soul here."

"Nevertheless, one of our professors has heard of your inquiry and really wants to meet with you," Wilson smiled.

---

1. "UBC" stands for the University of British Columbia, a public university in west Vancouver. Regent College is a seminary/graduate theology school that sits on the UBC grounds.

2. "Fraser" refers to Simon Fraser University, a public university in nearby Burnaby, just over fifteen miles (nearly 25 kilometers) east of Regent.

"And since it's a beautiful day outside, he was wondering if you'd like a picnic on the college grounds."

Jordan hesitated, overwhelmed by the unforeseen kindness. "I certainly don't object. I'm confused, but I don't object."

"Then I'll take you to him and leave you in his company," Wilson said, rising from his chair and gesturing toward the door. "Just one question: Can you handle hot, spicy food?"

"How hot and spicy?" asked Jordan. "And why?"

Jordan was expecting anyone other than the individual who sat on the oversized blanket spread on the manicured lawn. There, pressing currency into the hands of a delivery man, was a wizened-looking fellow clearly approaching eighty years of age. The navy-blue cardigan he wore complemented his white oxford shirt and grey slacks. His white hair tossed in the breeze that was blowing in from Point Grey. His eyes danced with joy even as they seemed to be somewhat cloudy. But there was no doubting his strength. His firm handshake impressed Jordan with its powerful grip.

"You must be Jordan!" he exclaimed. "I am Jim, Jim Packer. Please sit down, and accept my apologies for failing to rise. I find the older I get, the harder it is to get up from a comfortable position."

"Thank you, sir," gushed Jordan, scarcely able to fathom that he was about to have a picnic lunch with *the* J.I. Packer. "Is there anything I can do to spread things out?"

"Not to worry, young man," Packer insisted. "I just ordered some chicken vindaloo from my favorite Indian restaurant, and they know me well enough to deliver it here. Dr. Wilson, thank you so much for bringing Jordan."

"Enjoy your lunch. I'll speak to you later then," Wilson smiled before walking away.

After a prayer to bless the meal, Packer gave Jordan one of the boxed lunches and both men began eating. Jordan could not believe Packer could consume the vindaloo without so much as a gulp of the lemon soda provided. Packer ate his food as easily as he conversed, and Jordan felt he had steam coming out his own ears.

"So you desire to enter Regent for further study next year," said Packer, "but I assume there is a larger story behind your quest, young Jordan."

Jordan swallowed a piece of chicken, the temperature in his mouth reaching volcanic levels. Taking several gulps of soda to assuage the heat, he nodded. "At this time last year, I became a Christian believer. A friend of mine who was involved with InterVarsity[3] went through a rough time. His father was killed in a car wreck in Alberta, and the way Sam dealt with that made an impression on me. He cried, he grieved, don't get me wrong. But he also said he would see his dad again. I couldn't take that in, so our conversations led around to the resurrection of Jesus. I was skeptical, of course, but out of respect for Sam, I gave things a chance. I read books on it—crazy, because it wasn't my natural habit to read books about the Christian faith—and it hit me: If Jesus walked out of that tomb years ago, then it's not just a magic trick. If he was dead and then became alive again, there's nothing he can't do. And that means everything else about him is true. And if everything else about him is true, it meant I needed to live as though it is. That's what really led me to repent of my behavior and trust Jesus. All because a friend's dad had died." He paused. "That sounds strange that hope can come out of something so sad."

"I don't think it's as strange as that," Packer rejoined between bites of spicy chicken. "Affliction, I've found, is often the school in which God places us so we might learn to walk the next steps. It can be suffering we endure or a

---

3. InterVarsity is a Christian campus organization that ministers to students and faculty on college and university campuses in North America. Bible study and theological training are the hallmarks of InterVarsity's mission. For more information, see www.intervarsity.org

hardship someone else goes through and we learn through that. I'm speaking, of course, from the vantage point of seventy-six years of life. I am simply saying it is truer than we imagine."

Jordan wiped sweat from his brow, a tribute to the heat of the chicken. "I have no reason to disbelieve you, sir. I'm just very new to the Christian faith. I hope to learn through experience and that's part of why I am inquiring here."

"Well, that advice is always free," Packer answered with a twinkle in his eye. "I view it as a chisel in God's hands, by which He is sculpting our lives. Of course, we are weak, limited people, but that is why you and I must depend on Christ every day, and that dependence only will deepen as time goes on. The weaker we are, we lean more into Christ for His strength. And in a great irony, when we do that, the stronger we will grow."

"It sounds you're convinced of that because you've lived it," offered Jordan.

Packer looked to the cloudy sky and then back to Jordan. "It is," he replied, "and it began when I was seven years old in England. I was being chased by a school bully and I ran out into the street. Before I knew what happened, a bread van smashed into me and I fell to the pavement, my skull fractured. It was such immense, intense pain, and the surgeon had to delicately remove the broken shards of bone. That is why my head," and here Packer tapped the right side of his forehead, "looks like a hard-boiled egg when a spoon has cracked the shell. My recovery was difficult, and I was forbidden from participating in sports. But because of that, I turned to reading. Because I loved to read, I read classical literature. Because I read classical literature and loved school, I gained entrance to Oxford University. And because I was at Oxford, I wandered into a church there in which an elderly priest challenged his listeners if they were truly Christians. And because of that challenge, I gave my life to Jesus Christ that night. So yes, I have lived it—God shaping me in hope and blessing out of pain and suffering."

Rubbing his hands together, Packer looked intently at Jordan. "But you said you wish to learn more and that you are inquiring here. May I ask what has provoked this movement in the midst of your newfound faith?"

"It's actually something that arose this semester," said Jordan, "from a class I am taking. I was never one for philosophy, but when I trusted in Jesus I started considering the bigger questions of life. There was a 'selected topics' course in the philosophy department at Simon Fraser called 'The Meaning of Life', so I signed up for it. We've been discussing those very things I've been pondering more frequently. Why am I here? Why is life worth living? What is happiness? So the seminar has us swimming in the waters of Socrates, Plato, and others, plus theologians like Augustine and Aquinas. And what I've discovered is that I love facing those questions, but I need more. Dr. Hahn and fellow students will discuss things and throw around ideas and show respect to different views, but eventually one needs to identify where the answers are. And if the Bible gives God's answers, then even with going to Bible studies at school, I need to go deeper and really understand the Bible under people whose life is studying it and teaching it. If I'm following God, and the Bible is God's Word, it makes sense that I should understand it more to understand God's perspective on the meaning of life."

Packer smiled. "I'm very impressed, Jordan. You discovered your necessity for Scripture from your classroom environment! Not everyone would make that connection."

"I guess so," Jordan replied. "I hope so. I just hope I am heading down the right path, to commit to more study for three more years after graduation."

"I won't pretend to know fully the answer to that question," said Packer as he adjusted his spectacles. "Often, God will give us just enough direction for the next step of life when we are going about our ordinary business and following him. Yet what I do find encouraging is that you are a young Christian believer who has a high view of the Bible and yet also hungers to know more, and to know more of the Jesus the Bible reveals. That, incidentally, is the reason why I wanted to meet you. Dr. Wilson told me about your application and what you shared about yourself, so I have been looking forward to this."

"I'm very humbled, Dr. Packer," Jordan answered, stunned.

"It is a true privilege—one that should humble you greatly—to have been changed by the grace of God and have such a high view of His Word. There are a number of people who say they are Christians who don't," said Packer with a serious look on his face. "My prayer would be that you always have that passion. The Bible is the lifeline God throws in order that you remain connected to Him as He rescues you."

"It's encouraging, Dr. Packer," said Jordan, "that you seem to still have that passion."

"That is because God has been gracious to me. He stokes that passion," said Packer, "and His grace is everything and changes everything. God moved heaven and earth to save you and me when we could not lift a finger to save ourselves from eternal destruction. And by doing that, He is our Father who treasures us as His children."

Jordan felt a lump in his throat over the memory of loss. "I never thought of God much in that way. My own father died when I was ten." He wiped away a tear. "Cancer."

Tenderly, Packer reached across the space between them and placed his hand on Jordan's shoulder. "I am sorry to hear of his death. It is obvious you love him very much. I hope you will increasingly know God's own fatherly love for you."

"I know He has accepted me," Jordan offered.

"It is even more than that," Packer replied. "You are more than accepted; you are adopted by God, Who is your Father through what Jesus did by taking your place in death on the cross. To be accepted by God is a great thing, but to be loved and cared for by God is greater."

"I never thought of myself as adopted," Jordan mused as the breeze picked up and traffic buzzed along in the distance, "but the way you put it is undeniably beautiful."

"Adoption is the highest privilege of the good news you have embraced, Jordan my friend," Packer grinned broadly. "You were a traitor, and yet God has said to you, *'I have forgiven you, brought you in for supper, and given you my family name.'* There is no greater privilege than to have that love and know you are loved by God!"

Jordan took a sip of soda, wishing their conversation could go on and on. "I just hope I can continue believing that as you do so strongly."

"Faith is not about how strong your trust is, Jordan," said Packer, "but in Whom you place your trust. But there is nothing wrong with reinforcing your hope. And that comes by reminding yourself of your hope every day."

"Every day?"

"Yes, in six things you can tell yourself every day. Say them over and over to yourself first thing in the morning, last thing at night, as you sit in traffic, as you digest a snack, whenever your mind is free. Six things: *I am a child of God. God is my Father. Heaven is my home. Every day is one day nearer. My Savior is my brother. Every Christian is my brother, too.*"

Jordan closed his eyes and opened them, nodding slowly, drinking in the words. "I am a child of God. God is my Father. Heaven is my home. Every day is one day nearer. My Savior is my brother. Every Christian is my brother, too."

There was a long pause between the two men seated on the blanket, one young, one aged. Finally, Packer asked him, "Well, my friend. What do you think?"

Jordan looked around at the seminary building and then back at Packer himself. "I think my Father is showing me this feels like home."

JAMES INNELL PACKER (1926-2020) gained a well-deserved reputation for being one of the wisest leaders and writers in the Christian world of his time. Born in Gloucestershire, England, Packer embraced Jesus Christ as his Savior and Lord while studying at Oxford. An Anglican priest, professor, and tireless writer, Packer penned the classic *Knowing God* in 1973, which sold more than one million copies. With a great love for Biblical doctrine and careful reading of the Puritans, Packer's clear teaching and memorable writing style have made theology a delight for Christians the world over. In 1979, he and his family moved to Vancouver, where he taught at Regent College until his retirement. Throughout his life, Packer never let go of the precious truth that he and other believers are adopted and beloved by God.

BENJAMIN KWASHI

April 2007, Jos, Nigeria

The sounds of joy and celebration continued to pulse throughout the home well after the meal. Thanksgiving had been the rule of the day, which marked a full year since God's grace had rescued Gloria from further terror and brutality. As Ben danced across the floor with his children, he smiled with both happiness and relief.

"God is good!" sang the entire Kwashi clan as the evening went on, sons Rinji and Nanminen the loudest. "The Lord saves his people!"

Gloria and Ben joined hands and began dancing as their extended family continued the festivities. "What a day," said Gloria as she and Ben whirled around the room. "What a year of healing and provision from Jesus himself!"

"God is good, my wife," Ben grinned. "He is good indeed!"

Although the party showed no signs of abating, Ben and Gloria walked out to the courtyard. It was Ben's habit to walk through the area after nightfall, partially to say goodnight to their security guards, but tonight it was also to drink in the excitement Gloria felt as she greeted and gave a nighttime feeding to the animals in their ever-expanding zoo. It amazed Ben how much time Gloria gave to those she loved, whether human or animal. They practically had a safari within their compound. Goats constantly roamed over the grounds, chasing Ben's beloved group of pigeons. Sheep pattered around cows, their bleats mixing with the lowing of the cattle. Gloria walked to the sheep pen and poured another bucket of water into their drinking reservoir. Ben shook his head. *What a life,* he thought. *I am the archbishop, being a shepherd to the pastors who shepherd the Lord's people here in Jos, and there is Gloria showing the patience of a true shepherd.* Donkeys, monkeys, and pigs roamed around the yard, all the evidence of Gloria's desire to keep animals and bring joy into the lives of their birth and adopted children. Even some of Ben's pigeons fluttered about, always returning to their roosts in the darkness. *Give them a little sugar in their water,* Ben thought, *and pigeons will stay with you forever.*

There was much to give thanks for, Ben knew, for Gloria should not have survived the ordeal one year ago that day. The raiders had invaded their home, brutalized Gloria, and robbed them. Ben, at an event in London at the time, received word of the attack over the telephone. The memory of feeling so helpless, of praying passionately with no way of knowing if Gloria would survive, was still strong even as they gave thanks today for God's provision.

"Lost in your thoughts again, dear one?" asked Gloria as she drew next to her husband, threading her arm through his and looking at the happily munching animals.

Kissing the top of her head softly, Ben smiled and squeezed her arm in his. "As always, Mama, as always," he said, using Gloria's nickname of *Mama* tenderly. "Gratitude energizes the soul," he continued, "even as, at my age, my body is getting more and more tired."

"Come then," she declared, turning him back toward the house as they waved goodnight to the guards. "You could do with some sleep. Perhaps that will be our blessing for tonight."

Ben grinned with hope, although in less than three hours, they would find out that the blessing of slumber would not be theirs that night.

The smashing metal against steel woke Ben out of his sleep and he sat bolt upright in the bed. Gloria woke, as well, fumbling for her mobile phone on the bedside table. "Ben," she pleaded, "what's that?"

"Quiet," Ben replied gently. He crouched down and crawled over to the window, taking care not to trip over his nightwear. It was a clerical robe that an Egyptian priest friend had given him some time back. Since it was an old robe, Ben used it for his pajamas. Hearing a series of clicks behind him, he turned and saw Gloria on her phone.

"What are you doing?" he asked.

"Trying to get through to someone who can help," Gloria hissed, her fingers shaking.

Patting the air down in a calming gesture, Ben turned to the window and inched up until he could see the grounds. "Wait a minute, it may be nothing," he began, but as soon as he peeked outside, he knew better. The security lights were on, but no person could be seen. Below, he could hear footsteps. Scrambling back to his bed, Ben grabbed his own phone and began making calls, to friends, to fellow priests, to anyone who could listen.

"Ben!" Gloria whispered. She could hear the footsteps just outside the gates.

And yet, Ben sensed a calmness come over him, so definite it seemed as if he was wearing the calm like a cloak. Calling one of his priests, he quickly spoke into the phone, "Listen, it's Ben. We are under attack. If my time is up, don't be worried. I am at peace with going to see Jesus."

"Ben, what ... " came the reply, but Ben ended the call.

The footsteps were drawing nearer. Gloria crawled across the floor into the bathroom, shutting the door. *If she can get through to someone, I will thank God, and God will be good,* thought Ben. *And if she can't get through, God will still be good.*

159

"Gloria," he whispered. "I am ready. They might be Fulani[1]. If these guys come for me, they will shoot me, but I am ready."

The slamming sound below was deafening. Ben knew what must have happened. Whoever was coming had either captured or killed the security guards. The metal door was too thick for the sledgehammer, and Ben knew it was only a matter of time before they used a different contraption. *They will come prepared,* he told himself, *but I am prepared to meet them.*

A half-hour later, after the incessant slamming of the metal spike had finally pierced the door, the footsteps pounded through the house. The soldiers rushed up the stairs, bursting into the master bedroom.

And there, they saw the Nigerian archbishop on his knees in prayer. Ben had not stopped praying. He looked up and saw three men, knowing full well there were more outside. One man brandished a gun, one gripped a club, and the other held a knife. All three were unmasked. They did not care that Ben knew who had come to kill him.

The oldest of them waggled his pistol at Ben, shouting, "Man of God, get up and let's go! It's not time for praying now!"

Easing himself up to his feet, Ben raised his hands and said, "Fine," and walked out between two sets of soldiers. On and on Ben walked, praying, *Oh Lord, do not let them find Gloria. Do not let them harm my children. Do not let any children come out frightened and give themselves away.*

From up the stairs, he heard voices. "What are you doing? Let him go!" Stiffening, Ben knew that was his son Rinji and he lurched as the guards beat Rinji down as soon as he began to accost them. The click of cold metal in the

---

1. Fulani are tribal people in Saharan and west Africa, primarily Muslim by religion. Along with the Islamic terror group Boko Haram, Fulani are responsible for most of the attacks on Christians in Nigeria's Jos and Kaduna states.

darkness let Ben know they were holding a gun to his son's head. Then the patter of feet and the whimpering rage of son Nanminen followed. Ben heard a crack and knew one of the guards had punched him in the jaw.

And step after step, he went on, until he was outside.

There was a crowd of forty men surrounding him in the courtyard, while others kept guard on the periphery. Many of them looked to be in their twenties, young terrorists. Ben looked at several of them, a shiver going up his spine. They were wide-eyed, obviously drugged. The way they tucked their trousers into their boots, along with the knee-length robes they wore, showed Ben they were Fulani warriors. *Here to kill me in the name of Allah and for the glory of Islam,* Ben mused. *Lord, if they are going to kill me, let it not be in the house. Not in the presence of my family.*

One of them growled at him. "Listen, man of God. Give us money and we won't kill you!"

Ben shook his head, knowing it was a trap. "You know I don't have the money you would want!"

Another spat. "Three million naira[2]! Now!"

It was pointless. "You are too late," Ben replied. "You should have been here yesterday."

Then Ben heard someone shout from behind him. "Enough of this! Let's not kill him here."

"Then why did we bring him down?" slurred another who clutched an automatic rifle.

"Take him back upstairs!" came the reply. "Let's find his wife and kill him before her eyes! She shouldn't be too hard to find!"

And so they went back into the house, back up the stairs. It seemed to Ben that the house was shaking. Then he noticed one or two of the guards near him. They were shaking, twitching. Whether it was due to adrenaline,

---

2. The naira is the national currency of Nigeria. Three million naira at the time of this writing would be the equivalent of sixty-five hundred U.S. dollars or just over fifty-two hundred British pounds.

drugs, or the nerves of making an archbishop their next official kill, he did not know.

As they reached the second floor, Ben saw Rinji and Nanminen on the floor under armed guard. One soldier sneered as he pointed his rifle at the head of Rinji, who was face down with the warrior's foot pressed firmly into his back. Nanminen too was face down, his face disfigured from the punch to his jaw and bleeding from the mouth. *They broke his jaw when they came the last time and brutalized my Gloria,* Ben prayed, *so Lord, please let no bones be broken. Do not let him or any of the others be killed. If anyone is to die, let it be me.*

There were screams and yelps and Ben knew the Fulani soldiers had discovered Gloria, pulling her out and casting her roughly on the bedroom floor. The impact knocked the wind out of her, but as Ben padded up to her side, he could see her lips moving in silent prayer.

"Keep praying, Mama. Keep praying," were his words.

"Shut up, man of God!" barked the leader. "You be quiet now! The only sound to be made is the blast of our guns, the slashes of our knives, and the cracking of our clubs. Get down on the ground and we will kill you!"

This is it, thought Ben, acutely aware of the thump of his own heartbeat. *I am ready.*

"Please," he said to the leader just as the man cocked his pistol, "before you kill me, let me pray."

The man's eyes were bloodshot. His body oozed impatience. And yet for whatever reason, he said, "Okay. You can pray."

Ben knelt down on the floor next to Gloria. He had left his Bible on the bed, and in the earlier ruckus, it had dropped to the floor. He opened it, but couldn't make out the words without his glasses. *Thump-thump,* went his heart. He decided to ask another question, expecting to be torn apart by bullets just for asking.

"May I please get my reading glasses?" Ben asked calmly. "They are on the bedside table here."

"Get them and hurry!" ordered the leader, and Ben crept to the table, plucked his half-moon spectacles, and slid back toward his wife. Gloria was shaking but praying silently, her lips moving. Even when one of the guards struck her with the butt of his rifle, she flinched but didn't stop praying.

Ben knelt on the big red rug, put on his glasses, and opened his brown leather Bible. *What to say at a time like this?* Ben asked. And then he knew. The twenty-third Psalm.

"The Lord is my shepherd," Ben prayed. "I shall not want ... " He pressed his hands together and he continued, going on to "Even though I walk through the valley of the shadow of death, I will fear no evil."

Worried the soldiers might hit him, Ben slid forward, prostrating himself on the floor, his Bible before him, his hands atop his head. Footsteps were thudding around them.

Ben couldn't bring himself to look. Continuing to pray, he lost track of time. He could smell the sweat and odor of the soldiers. They were still in the room. *Why haven't they killed me,* he wondered.

He felt a hand on his. Gloria's. Her voice was warm and steady. "Shh. Just pray." She was praying silently, but Ben could read her lips as she entreated God. *Lord, let there be no bloodshed tonight. Lord, there shall be no bloodshed. Deny them the opportunity for bloodshed.*

Seconds dripped into minutes. *How long will this go on,* wondered Ben. Nobody touched him. Then the room went completely silent.

Lord, Ben prayed, *let them kill me alone, not Gloria. Only me, Lord, for the sake of the children.*

All he could hear was the beating of his heart against the rug. With each thump, he expected it to be his last.

Why have they not touched me, he asked silently. *Why have they not killed me?*

He heard, barely, Gloria whisper next to him. He couldn't make out her words, but she grew as animated as she could be with death a slender thread away. Then Ben heard them. Footsteps. They moved around the room. No voices. Just footsteps. Many footsteps. Then they faded. Then footsteps again. One set of footsteps. And they stopped in front of Ben as he lay face down on the floor.

My hour has come, Ben told himself. *This is it.*

Only there was no shot ringing out. What was going on?

Slowly, Ben lifted his head off the ground and beheld a pair of legs. No army trousers. No flowing Fulani robe. Bare legs. *I know those,* Ben marveled. He looked up at the person in front of him.

It was Rinji!

"Rinji!" Ben whispered, scarcely believing his eyes. How was he there? He had been under armed guard! "Son, what are you doing here?"

In a voice choking with emotion, Rinji replied, "Daddy, they are all gone."

Scrambling to his feet, then helping Gloria up, Ben stared at the bedroom. Not a single Fulani warrior was there. No guns, no knives, no clubs. *I never heard them go,* Ben marveled to himself. *Why am I still alive?*

"Rinji," he said, grasping his son by his shoulders, "are you sure?"

"Yes, Daddy," came the response. "No one is left. Come, let's go tell everyone else!"

Ben and Gloria ran throughout the house. It was completely empty of all invaders. Running to the gatehouse, he freed the security guards. They had been beaten, bloodied, and locked in, but they were very much alive! Ben turned back to the house, which had suddenly become an epicenter of sound and rejoicing. Nigerian military and other police had shown up too late, but it hardly mattered.

"God be praised!" Ben shouted happily as he found Gloria back in the house.

"Let's wake the children up!" she sang loudly. "By God's mercy, they must have slept through the whole thing! If they had wakened, they would have screamed the place down. We have all been spared."

"Our Savior intervened!" Ben danced, his hands raised. Soon the other children, both their own and those they had adopted, rushed into the living area from all corners of the house and heard the story again.

"Praise the Lord always!" they shouted.

"Glory to God with all my heart!" came the cry of others, and the singing and dancing began again.

It would not end for several hours later.

"I should have died," Ben said later as he stood outside, his arms around Gloria. "But here I am, thanks be to God. You prayed and I am still here."

"All I remember," Gloria smiled, "is as we were face down—right before I believed they would shoot you—I heard a man come in. His voice was strong yet gentle and he said, 'Okay, drop this thing. Get out now.' And I'm sure that's when they left. I can't explain it."

Ben shook his head in amazement. "There is nothing to explain, but plenty to praise. What those soldiers saw, only eternity will reveal to us. It might have been a call on their radios. It might well have been an angel who walked in and ordered them out. That is not the issue. But this is: Let us consider how to respond in love."

"I already have an idea," said Gloria as she hugged her husband close. "And I think you'll love it, because we can demonstrate the love of Christ that has been shown to us. And I'm so happy I still have you to do this with me."

"For as long as God gives me," Ben replied, "for I know one day I will die. Gun shot, car crash, air crash, whatever befalls me ... but until that day let us live for Him! Because we have a Gospel worth living for, and we have a Gospel worth dying for!"

BENJAMIN KWASHI (born 1955) has served as the Archbishop of Jos in the Anglican Church of Nigeria, as well as the secretary of the Global Anglican Future Conference (GAFCON). Living in Jos, the capital of Nigeria's Plateau State, Ben has ministered to Nigerian Christians on the front line of persecution and death, as Fulani militants and Boko Haram terrorists seek to impose hardline Islamic rule. Ben has trained many priests faithfully in Scripture and theology to be effective and godly pastors. He and his wife Gloria have six children and also house over sixty orphans, providing health care, education, and sustenance to them, all while surviving several attacks and attempts on their lives. With a passion to see their countrymen come to love Jesus Christ, Ben and Gloria show the forgiveness of God in response to even the worst attacks. After the events of this story, Ben paid for the scholarships of over seventy Muslim children to come to their schools for a robust education and exposure to the Gospel, a remarkable and stunning act of compassion and love as they seek to serve Christ.

FACT FILES

What Does the Future Hold?

This series of books has taken us through many people, places, and events. But if we included everyone, these books would be way too large! It is good to think of church history as a treasure chest. In this series we examined a significant amount of the jewels in that chest. Not the entire haul. I hope your curiosity has been sparked and that you want to encounter more people–bold yet flawed–who follow Jesus. One thing is certain and that is church history is not done.

Here is a final word about where Christianity might be heading. When Jesus told His disciples in Acts 1 that they would take the good news "to the ends of the earth", that was an undertaking that would go on until the end of human history. Now in the twenty-first century, where does Christianity stand, and where is it going?

Chances are we could look at the last four centuries and wonder if the Church will even have a future. After the conflicts coming out of the Protestant Reformation, a number of thinkers in Europe began speaking out in favor of a more distant view of God. Leaders of the Enlightenment put forth the idea that while the world was created by God, after creation God left it alone to run on natural scientific laws. They believed our purpose as humans was not to be saved from our sinful condition or opposition to God, but that we needed to pursue the truth found in scientific observation. To them, the world revealed what is normal, so that is how we discovered truth, not in primarily looking to God. The French Revolution went further, pushing the influence of the Church to the margins of society. A growing secularization in Europe continues to this day.

Weekly worship attendance is extraordinarily low.[1] In Germany, the nation that launched the Reformation, only about 10 per cent of the population attends church once a week. In the United Kingdom, that metric stands at 8 per cent, and Sweden sits at 6 per cent.

Even with North America's higher attendance rates— where Canadians attend church weekly at a 20 per cent clip and the United States reports a rate of 36 per cent—a growing number of people do not identify with any religion, called the "nones". In 2020, 64 per cent of Americans identified as *"Christian"*[2] while the religious *nones* are at 30 per cent. By 2070, researchers believe we could see an even split between Christians and nones in America. There is no doubt the Holy Spirit works powerfully as he sees fit, and trends can reverse. But it does demonstrate—for now—a religious landscape that is quite different.

We should remind ourselves, though, that Jesus never said we were to take the Gospel to Europe and America only. In truth, Christianity is not shrinking in number or geographic spread, but rather moving its center point of influence.[3] In the early days of the First World War (think 1915-ish), 80 per cent of the world's Christians dwelt in Europe and North America. Now that stands at 40 per cent. For some time, there have been more Christians living south of the equator than north of it, and there is no reason to think that trend will change. One out of four Christians *in the entire world* lives in Africa, and experts

---

1. All statistics culled from the Pew Research Center's most recent report at https:/ www.pewresearch.org/religion/2018/06/13/how-religious-commitment-varies-by-country-among-people-of-all-ages/

2. It should go without saying that this is an identity statement and does not reflect whether someone is necessarily a committed follower of Jesus Christ with a lively daily faith. This statistic and ones that follow are from a more recent Pew Research initiative from https://www.pewresearch.org/religion/2022/09/13/modeling-the-future-of-religion-in-america/

3. I reference Wes Granberg-Michaelson's excellent article from the *Washington Post* in the bibliography at the end of the book. These gleanings that follow are from that article.

believe that number could go as high as 40 per cent by the end of this decade! Latin America is seeing tremendous growth among Christians, and Brazil has more Pentecostal/ Charismatic believers than any other nation on earth.

The Far East is a region teeming with new Gospel life. Christianity has grown at twice the rate of Asia's population over the last century. Even Communist nations like China and North Korea have dedicated underground churches where people worship in secret. And the impact of worldwide immigration cannot be ignored. Asian and African believers who move to Europe and America bring their spiritual vitality to these new landscapes.[4]

The growth of the Christian faith all over the world, however, does not guarantee easy days for followers of Jesus. The Church that serves her Lord will be an *enduring Church* and believers will have to go through trials, and persecution. Followers of Jesus in nations like Uzbekistan are threatened with ultimatums if they have converted from Islam to the Christian faith. Family members force new believers to choose between belonging in the family or being expelled from the home if they choose Christ. In Tanzania, pastors are beaten or slashed with knives because of their love for Christ. In North Korea and China, police raid worship services and harass or imprison ministers, yet Christians faithfully share their hope in Christ with others.

The Church that endures will ultimately be the Church victorious. Though Satan will attack God's people throughout the ages, the Lord gives His people both the power to endure and great blessing after that endurance. In Revelation 7, the apostle John is given a vision in which he sees Christians who have come through intense persecution and vicious attacks and notes that "They have

---

4. For more on the impact of immigration, and the stance that we as believers should have toward its blessings, see chapter 20 in my *Tough Issues, True Hope: A Concise Journey Through Christian Ethics* (Ross-shire, UK: Christian Focus Publications, 2020).

washed their robes and made them white in the blood of the Lamb. Therefore, they are before the throne of God, and serve Him day and night in His temple; and He Who sits on the throne *will shelter them with His presence.* They shall hunger no more, neither thirst anymore; the sun shall not strike them, nor any scorching heat. For the Lamb in the midst of the throne will be their shepherd, and He will guide them to springs of living water, and God will wipe away every tear from their eyes" (Revelation 7:14b-17).

This is a message of hope that we who follow Christ must constantly keep in our minds and hearts. Although we may go through great hardship, we have a Savior who rescues His people out of adversity (1 Kings 1:29). And speaking of our Savior, we can always rely on His precious promises to us: "I will build My Church, and the gates of hell will not prevail against it ... And behold, I am with you always, to the end of the age" (Matthew 16:18b; Matthew 28:20).

Even though this series of books has come to an end, the story has not. The story continues, and we can have confidence that God is the One who guides it on to the end. Also, you get to play a role in the continuation of this story; your life is part of what lies ahead in the future. What you do matters tremendously in the unfolding drama of Jesus' people. And through it all, we can be assured of the presence of a global family of believers, for "there shall always be a Church on earth, to worship God according to His will."[5]

---

5. From chapter 25, section 5 of the Westminster Confession of Faith.

WHERE WE GET OUR INFORMATION

Bailey, E.K. and Warren Wiersbe. *Preaching in Black and White: What We Can Learn From Each Other.* Grand Rapids, MI: Zondervan, 2003.

Bibi, Asia and Anne-Isabelle Tollet. *Blasphemy: A Memoir (Sentenced to Death Over a Cup of Water).* Chicago, IL: Chicago Review Press, 2013.

Bonhoeffer, Dietrich. *The Cost of Discipleship,* rev. paperback ed. New York, NY: Collier Books, 1963.

Bonhoeffer, Dietrich. *Letters and Papers from Prison.* New York, NY: MacMillan, 1953.

Boyd, Andrew. *Neither Bomb Nor Bullet: Benjamin Kwashi, Archbishop on the Front Line.* London, UK: Monarch Books, 2019.

Burson, Scott R. and Jerry Walls. *C.S. Lewis and Francis Schaeffer: Lessons for a New Century from the Most Influential Apologists of Our Time.* Downers Grove, IL: InterVarsity Press, 1998.

Dilley, Andrea Palpant. "Meet the Women Apologists". *Christianity Today.* April 2015, 34.

Elliot, Elisabeth. *Through Gates of Splendor.* Carol Stream, IL: Tyndale House Publishers, rev. ed. 2005.

Gonzalez, Justo. *The Story of Christianity, vol. 2: From the Reformation to the Present Day.* New York, NY: Harper & Row, 1985.

Keller, Timothy. *The Reason for God: Belief in an Age of Skepticism.* New York, NY: Penguin Books, 2008.

Levine, Ellen. *Darkness Over Denmark: The Danish Resistance and the Rescue of the Jews.* New York, NY: Scholastic, 2000.

Lewis, Clive Staples. *Mere Christianity.* New York, NY: Macmillan Publishers, 1977 (mass market paperback).

Linnemann, Eta. *Historical Criticism of the Bible: Methodology or Ideology?* Tr. By Robert W. Yarbrough. Grand Rapids, MI: Baker Book House, 1990.

McGrath, Alister, ed. *The Christian Theology Reader, Third Edition.* Hoboken, NJ: Wiley-Blackwell, 2006.

Murray, Iain H. *J.C. Ryle: Prepared to Stand Alone.* Edinburgh, UK: Banner of Truth Trust, 2016.

Noll, Mark. *Turning Points: Decisive Moments in the History of Christianity.* Grand Rapids, MI: Baker Books, 1997.

Olson, Roger. *The Story of Christian Theology.* Downers Grove, IL: InterVarsity Press, 1999.

Political Theology Network. https://politicaltheology.com/francis-grimke-an-african-american-witness-in-reformed-political-theology/ accessed March 2023.

Poulsen, Soren Toftgaard. "The Pastor of Vederso". http://www.kulturarv.dk/1001fortaellinger/en_GB/hoerbylunde accessed March 2023.

Robinson, Haddon. *Biblical Preaching: The Development and Delivery of Expository Messages* (3rd ed.). Grand Rapids, MI: Baker Academics.

Ryle, John Charles. *Expository Thoughts on the Gospels: St. Matthew and St. Mark.* Cambridge, UK: James Clarke & Co. Ltd., reprint 1983.

Schaeffer, Edith. *The Tapestry.* Waco, TX: Word Publishers, 1984.

Shelley, Bruce. *Church History in Plain Language.* Nashville, TN: Thomas Nelson, 1995.

"Stories of Christian Martyrs: Chester A. 'Chet' Bitterman III". https://www.persecution.com/stories/stories-of-christian-martyrs-chester-a-chet-bitterman-iii/

Stott, John. *Between Two Worlds: The Art of Preaching in the Twentieth Century.* Grand Rapids, MI: Eerdmans, 1982.

Strobel, Lee. *The Case for Christ.* Grand Rapids, MI: Zondervan, 1998.

ten Boom, Corrie. *The Hiding Place.* Chosen Books, 1971.

"Uzbekistan". *The Voice of the Martyrs.* October 2022, 4-15.

Thomas, Geoff. "J. Alec Motyer" https://banneroftruth.org/us/resources/articles/2000/j-alec-motyer/

Walton, Robert C. *Chronological and Background Charts of Church History.* Grand Rapids, MI: Zondervan, 1986.

Woodson, Carter, ed. *The Works of Francis Grimke.* Washington, D.C.: The Associated Publishers, 1942.

Yarbrough, Robert W. "Eta Linnemann: Friend or Foe of Scholarship?" The Master's Seminary Journal, vol. 8, issue 2 (Fall 1997), 163-189.

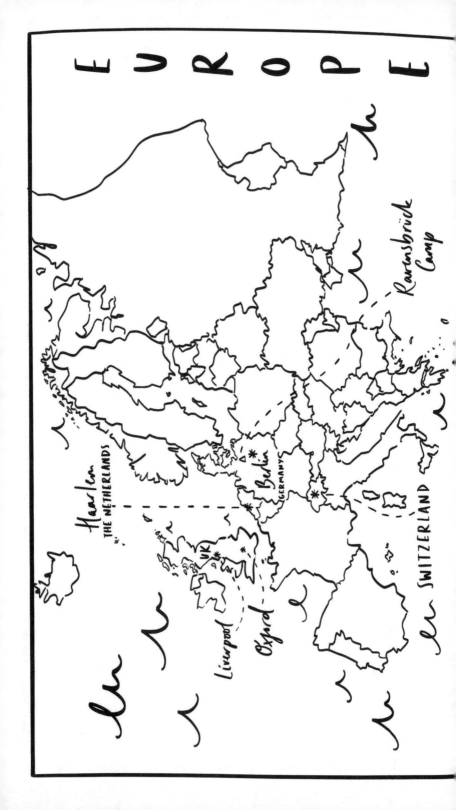

Christian Focus Publications publishes books for adults and children under its four main imprints: Christian Focus, CF4K, Mentor and Christian Heritage. Our books reflect our conviction that God's Word is reliable and Jesus is the way to know him, and live for ever with him.

Our children's publication list covers pre-school to early teens. We also publish personal and family devotional titles, biographies and inspirational stories that children will love.

From pre-school board books to teenage apologetics, we have it covered!

Christian Focus Publications Ltd,
Geanies House, Fearn, Ross-shire,
IV20 1TW, Scotland,
United Kingdom.

Find us at our web page:
www.christianfocus.com